Publisher and Supplier:
Richemont Craft School, CH-6006 Lucerne

Product photographs: Richemont Craft School, Lucerne
Still life: R. Heeb, Lucerne
Cover: R. Spengler, Berne
Illustrations: M. Nuber, Kastanienbaum
Concept/Authors: Heads of Department, Richemont Craft School
Print: Abächerli Druck AG, CH-6061 Sarnen

Printed in Switzerland

ISBN 3-905720-22-1

Mixed Sources
Product group from well-managed
forests and other controlled sources
www.fsc.org Cert no. IMO-COC-027720
© 1996 Forest Stewardship Council
FSC

Swiss
Bakery

Richemont Craft School

Swiss bakery

A feature of the Swiss bread and bakery assortment is the almost unlimited variety of diverse products. The craftsmanship used in the careful processing of high quality raw materials has received attention from far over the Swiss border, which in connection with the International orientated training and further education activities of the Richemont Craft School, has led to the worldwide recognition of the professional standing of the Swiss baker, confectioner and confiseur. With the book "Swiss Bakery" which was firstly published by the Richemont Craft School in 1983 a basic work is available which addresses everyone interested in bread and bakery products.

In the three national languages of German, French and Italian and supplemented with the editions in English and Japanese the book is registered in great demand. Due to this requirement the reprints allow the authors of the Richemont Craft School to periodically update the new editions, to include the latest technical processing developments, and to bring the basic recipes up-to-date.

The great success of this book however, surely based on its application in the workplace.

Walter Boesch
Director

In addition to Swiss Bakery, various specialist craftbooks and EDP-articles are also available from the Richemont Craft School.

Tutilo Tafel
It is the oldest illustration of bread in Switzerland. The scene is carved on an ivory board which is found in the monastry of St. Gallen and dates back to the 9th or 10th Century. The lower scene shows the Holy Gallus giving bread to the bears as a payment for collecting wood.

From the history of bread and bakery craft

Dr. sc. techn. h.c. Max Währen

According to the latest research the bakery oven is approximately 7800 years old. In Asia Minor, in Tschatal Hüyük, an oven has been found dating back to between 5900 BC and 5700 BC. The often acclaimed fact that the Egyptians discovered bread is therefore false. It is however true that the Egyptians did have bakeries with bakery directors between the years 3000 and 2700 BC. It is from this time in history that the oldest known bakers' name originates. The name is "Fire Hook" and comes from the ancient Egyptian hyroglyphic script for the word baker. The symbol consisted of an arrow shaped hook, which is what the baker used to draw the bread pots out of the fire with. By the year 2000 BC the Egyptians had developed 16 different types of bread products, of which the author has been able to ident-ifly 15. The author has also been able to identify 30 different cake and bread products from the year 1200 BC, it is however possible that the Egyptians had as many as 48 different types.

In old Mesopotania, the land of Abraham, the trade of baker was regarded as a gift from God. Between 3000 and 1200 BC, 59 types and forms of bread were available. Also in Europe, in Bulgaria and Bohemia, bakery ovens have been discovered dating back to 4800 BC. The author has also found sour bread in Switzerland dating back to 3700—3600 BC, as well as an undamaged bread dating back to 3530 BC. During the so-called "Urn-field era" sour bread even had a religious importance. The dead were cremated on big bonfires and their ashes were stored in urns. The author has discovered many examples of sour bread next to the burried urns which date back to 1200 BC. Another undamaged bread has been discovered in Switzer-land from the year 1000—900 BC. It is made of wheat flour has a diameter of 10.5 cm, is 2.5 cm thick, weighs 79 g and can now be seen in the Museum of Yverdon.

The Bakers trade in Switzerland can be traced back to between 613 and 623 AD. In the plan of the Monastry of St. Gallen. 820 AD, three bakeries are drawn. From 1000 AD a list of the foods to be blessed in the Monastry named 19 types of bread, of which a few are however identical.

The oldest bakers guild was founded in 14 AD in Rome. The extention and a thorough modernisation followed in the year 100 AD, whereby members received duties and priviliges. The number of members was restricted to 100. By the 4th Century there were 254 public baker-ies, which were something like State bakeries, because the State pro-vided free bread for approximately 150 000 people.

In Switzerland bakers guilds were established in Basel (1256), Zürich (1331), St. Gallen (1362) Luzern (1371) and in Freiburg (1389).

What you have just read is only a small part of the long history of breadmaking. Life was not always easy in the Swiss bakery trade. Even in the 14th or 15th Century, bakers had great problems with find-ing staff and with trade wars of all kinds. But they overcame them with skill, patience and always came up with new ideas.

The reason for my looking back on the history of baking is because I am convinced that the baker should be aware of the traditions of his trade. In conjuction with this awareness is the need to maintain these traditions, which thereby give an in-sight into the cultural aspects of our country. With this I would once more like to say that I hope that the fruits of this book are enjoyed by many people.

Cereals and flour – the most important raw materials

The production of good quality bread and pastry, besides excellent technical knowledge, requires a careful and skilled processing of prime quality raw materials. The flour in particular must be of uniform and stable quality and must have good baking qualities. For the purpose of securing regular supplies, domestic bread grain production is promoted by the guarantee to the producers that all the grain they produce will be taken over by the government at a fixed price. It is required that 85% of the grain processed by the milling industry (about 430 000 tons annually) be domestic. It therefore requires a domestic cultivation of high quality wheat. The cultivation and testing of new varieties is undertaken by the Federal Research Centres. Thus it is ensured that the quality of the wheat meets the requirements of the producers and manufacturers. By the classification of the wheat varieties into different price-classes and by payment according to quality, bread grain cultivation is influenced in such a way as to secure the production of flour with good baking characteristics.

The supply of bread grain

(Article 23 of the Federal Constitution)
The laws concerning the supply of bread grain in our country are embodied in the Federal Constitution. These basically concern:

The importation of bread grain

Grain traders and commercial mills are the only companies entitled to import bread grain. The Federal Department of Agriculture also has the authority to import bread grain, for the replenishment of national reserve stocks.

Bread grain reserves

A distinction is made between the basic reserve stocks (100 000 tons) and the additional reserve stocks (360 000 tons). The latter being due to Switzerland's solitary international position. Together with these stocks and an intensified domestic production the nation's supply of bread grain is secured, even in times of war or other emergencies.

The promotion of domestic bread grain cultivation

The government takes over all the grain from the producers. A measure which provides the farmers with the guarantee that they will be able to sell their grain, provided that quality specifications are fulfilled. The purchasing prices are graduated according to the quality of the harvest as well as the milling and baking properties of the grain. These prices are fixed by the government on a yearly basis, prior to the harvest. The prices are fixed in such a manner as to cover the costs of production.
To promote the cultivation of bread grain in disadvantaged areas (climatic and topographical disadvantages) the government pays production incentives to farmers in such areas. Today, about two-thirds of all grain producers are getting such incentives. Some 40% of the land cultivated with bread grain is located within disadvantaged areas.
For testing purposes, the government is also promoting the breeding of new varieties and is supporting correlative tests and research activities.

Allocation of domestic grain to the mills

In order to secure the domestic production of bread grain, the commercial mills are obliged to purchase the grain at the costprice from the government.

Cereal Breeding

The Swiss Federal Research Stations for Agronomy in Changins/Nyon and Reckenholz/Zurich are entrusted with the breeding of wheat varieties which are adapted to our climatic conditions. The aim is to produce a wheat variety which is resistant to diseases, is hardy, has a high grain yield and prosseses optimal milling and baking properties. After the selection of suitable parental varieties, some hundred crosses are made and from about 300 000 descendant plants the most promising lines are selected for preliminary trials and for further extensive tests over the following three years on different locations. Thus it may take between 12 and 15 years from the crossing to the final registration of a new variety.

Variety Testing

The testing of all bread cereal varieties also belongs the duties of the Research Stations. Only those varieties which have proved their agronomic suitability and their milling and baking quality over a period of at least three years are set on the Official List of Cereal Varieties. The classification into the price classes is made on the basis of the agronomic and technical values of the new varieties. The Swiss Seed Growers Association ensures that the variety stays pure and that only certified seeds are sold on the market.

Official List of wheat varieties

Variety	Country of origin	Year of registration
Winter wheat (class 1)		
Arina	CH	1981
Eiger	CH	1980
Ramosa	CH	1989
Tamaro	CH	1992
Spring wheat (class 1)		
Calanda	CH	1979
Albis	CH	1983
Remia	CH	1986
Lona	CH	1991
Winter wheat (class 2)		
Zenith	CH	1969
Forno	CH	1986
Garmil	CH	1987
Boval	CH	1990
Galaxie	F	1991
Asiago*	I	1985
Spring wheat (class 2)		
Frisal	CH	1987

* for Ticino only

Bread Grain Growing in Switzerland

Wheat

The acreage of bread cereals, (i.e. wheat, rye and spelt) amounts to approximately 100 000 hectares, of which wheat takes up 85%.
The wheat growing areas of Waadt and the Bernese Middle Land are the main grain growing areas of Switzerland, as can be seen from the following graph.

Bread grain deliveries / percentage according to Cantons (1991):

below 5%: LU/SZ/ZG/SO/BS/BL/SH/SG/GR/TI/VS/NE/GE
5 to 10%: TG/ZH/FR/AG
10 to 20%: BE
over 25%: VD

Rye

Rye does not need good soil or climatic conditions, it shows a good winter hardiness as well as a good resistance to diseases. As a self-compatible cereal rye is well suited to crop rotation which is important to our agricultural system, being cereal crop orientated. The acreage of rye is steadily decreasing, and has reached a surface area of approx. 5000 ha. With increasing yields the supply more than meets the demands, and some rye has to be sold cheaply as fodder.

Spelt

In the marginal zones of the grain growing areas there is a high annual rainfall. Here spelt is grown as opposed to wheat, due to its ruggedness and its resistance to diseases. Spelt is mainly grown in the Cantons of Berne, Lucerne and Aargau. The acreage amounts to 2000 hectares, and the grain is used for the production of speciality flours (e. g. for flat cakes).

Mixtures

The growing of wheat and rye together as a mixture has lost its importance almost completely. The acreage today only covers some hundred hectares, furthermore, mixtures with more than 50% rye will be classified as rye at delivery.

Test field of the Swiss Federal Research Station for Agronomy Zurich-Reckenholz.

Apart from the study of agronomic characteristics, the examination of milling and baking properties are of utmost importance in the cultivation and the selection of new wheat varieties.

Swiss Bread Grain Production

The national agricultural production programme's aim is to be self-sufficient. This requires a domestic production of 70–80% of the total Bread Grain consumed.

Grain delivery (in tons) to the Federal Government

Year	grain for milling	sprouted grain	total delivery	self-supply for farmers
1974	385 200	—	385 200	28 240
1975	277 200	37 540	314 740	24 840
1976	217 920	160 900	378 820	23 190
1977	281 930	10 470	292 400	24 190
1978	370 170	14 230	384 400	24 130
1979	395 870	8 800	404 670	22 470
1980	364 090	1 930	366 020	21 450
1981	364 855	16 075	380 930	20 120
1982	219 990	181 420	401 410	21 120
1983	404 150	320	404 470	20 200
1984	542 720	21 750	564 470	
1985	508 156	192	508 348	
1986	460 575	835	461 410	
1987	429 399	7 055	436 454	
1988	531 412	411	531 823	
1989	623 160	1 757	624 917	
1990	536 425	1 815	538 240	
1992	574 873	6 236	581 109	

Percentages of the wheat varieties

From the volume of domestic wheat production the minimum amount of grain to be taken over by the millers is worked out. With a total amount of flour milled of approx. 450 000 tonnes the inland fraction lies between 60 and 85%. In order to assure a good flour quality an appropriate assortment of different varieties is required. Although the growing conditions for wheat are usually not favourable in Switzerland the quality of the Swiss varieties meets the international standards. When testing the new varieties the Federal Grain Administration usually makes a comparison with imported wheat from the USA and Canada. The following figures are taken from the quality investigations by the Swiss School of Baking Richemont, Lucerne, and reflect the averages of the harvests 1983 and 1984. Only a selection of the varieties tested is shown.

Variety

class 1	1991 %	1992 %	class 2	1991 %	1992 %
Arina	70,8	73,3	Zenith	2,3	1,5
Eiger	1,4	0,8	Forno	7,3	5,0
Sardona	0,5	0,4	Garmil	1,6	2,7
Albis	1,1	2,0	Ramosa	0,2	—
Remia	0,6	0,2	Boval	5,8	5,9
Frisal	1,7	1,1	Galaxie	1,6	1,4

The Swiss Milling Industry

Protection of its' interests by the Federal Government

Legal measures have been taken to protect the Swiss milling industry and to ensure a reasonable distribution of milling plants throughout the whole country.

The import monopoly

Of flour by the Federal Government prevents unwanted competition from foreign countries.

The compensation of milling fees

ensures the survival of medium and small mills.

The balance of transport costs

For the distribution of inland cereals secures equal prices for all mills, irrespective of location and accessability.

Price control

The Federal Government controls the prices of bakery flours and bread. The Associations are obliged to report any changes of prices to the Federal Department of Agriculture as well as to allow examination of records on the course of business in both milling and baking industry.

Structure of the Milling Industry

Trade mills

They are responsible for the industrial processing of bread cereals and for the subsequent trading of the cereal products.

No of trade mills (as at 1992)	output in tons	share of market in percent
51 small mills	up to 500	2,1
51 medium mills	up to 6000	23,9
19 large mills	over 6000	74,0

Grain imports

Country of origin	Bread wheat in tons 1991	1992
Canada	40327	32651
USA	25987	11607
France	12440	15884
Austria	131	131
Federal Rep. of Germany	294	35
Italy	224	174
Argentina	1480	1408
Saudi-Arabia	13929	6018
Australia	–	–
Various countries	60	445
Total	94872	68353

Production of various wheat flour types in relation to the total flour output (in %)

Year	white flour	half-white flour	dark flour	special flour incl. rye flour
1981/82	34,2	38,7	18,6	8,5
1982/83	34,6	37,9	18,8	8,7
1983/84	33,8	38,3	19,0	8,9
1984/85	33,5	38,1	19,2	9,2
1985/86	32,5	39,1	19,1	9,3
1986/87	43,5	27,5	19,0	10,0
1987/88	43,6	27,4	18,7	10,3
1988/89	44,2	26,6	18,5	10,7
1989/90	44,4	26,6	18,5	10,5
1990/91	44,8	26,3	18,6	10,2
1991/92	46,5	25,7	18,4	9,4

Included in the figures is the flour destined for export (half-white flour) as well as the flour used for industrial purposes. Thus the flour used for direct human consumption in Switzerland is 10000–12000 tons less than the figures above.

The figures used, together with the other data for milling output, have been taken from the statistical annual report of the Swiss Millers Association.

Calculation of bread consumption per person/day: 1990–1992 (acc. to production)

	1990	1991	1992	
Flour output	365 183,3 t	354 903,9 t	358 565,3 t	
Flour for home-baking	+ 4 000,0 t	+ 4 000,0 t	+ 4 000,0 t	
Export surplus	− 3 897,3 t	− 4 393,8 t	− 5 419,0 t	
Total flour use	365 286,0 t	354 510,1 t	357 146,3 t	
Population	6,751 Mio.	6,832 Mio.	6,905 Mio.	
Flour consumption per person/year	54,1 kg	51,9 kg	51,7 kg	100%
minus:				
Confectionery items	8,1 kg	7,9 kg	7,7 kg	
Biscuit industry	4,5 kg	4,7 kg	4,9 kg	
Soup	0,5 kg	0,5 kg	0,5 kg	
Baby food	0,1 kg	0,1 kg	0,1 kg	
Detail sale	6,6 kg 19,8 kg	7,1 kg 20,2 kg	7,2 kg 20,4 kg	39%
Netto flour use for bread and baking products	34,3 kg	31,7 kg	31,3 kg	61%
Consumption of bread and baking products per person/day	**145 g**	**134 g**	**132 g**	
Consumption of bread and baking products incl. similar bread products per person/day	**147 g**	**136 g**	**134 g**	
Consumption of bread and baking products incl. similar bread broducts per person/year	**53,6 kg**	**49,6 kg**	**49,0 kg**	

From grain to flour

The wheat kernel

The wheat kernel is the fruit of the wheat plant. From the morphological point of view all the fruits of other cereals and grasses are similar, which means that they can roughly be subdivided into bran, starchy endosperm and germ. These three main parts of the fruit or caryopsis are kept tightly together and differ widely in their chemical composition. However, although the other cereals and grasses are similar to wheat, they too differ greatly in their chemical compositions:

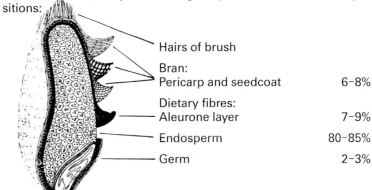

Hairs of brush	
Bran: Pericarp and seedcoat	6–8%
Dietary fibres: Aleurone layer	7–9%
Endosperm	80–85%
Germ	2–3%

Functions of the parts of the grain

The wheat bran

makes up approximately 7% of the kernel (excluding the aleurone layer). It is composed of several morphological layers which mainly consist of cellulose and hemicelluloses which have an important function as roughage in our nutrition. The seedcoat is a part of the bran. It prevents the water from entering into the starchy endosperm and in addition it contains fungicidal and bactericidal substances which act as a physiological barrier to the growth of microorganisms.

The aleurone layer

makes up approximately 7% of the kernel. This layer is mainly found together with the bran fractions in the mill. Its protein concentration is about 14% and it contains roughly 4% fat. Most minerals and trace elements in the wheat kernel occur within that aleurone layer. It also contains several vitamins.

The starchy endosperm

makes up approximately 83% of the wheat kernel. It contains 100% of the kernel's starch and more than 70% of the total protein. During germination it supplies all the nutrients to the growing germ.

The germ

makes up approximately 3% of the wheat kernel. The germ has the highest concentration of proteins (27%), of fats (9%) and of some vitamins. It also contains considerable amounts of minerals and trace elements.

Separation of bran and endosperm

The design and complexity of the milling machines depends greatly on the flour types required — for example whole wheat flour can be produced simply by grinding the wheat into the required particle size, because no separation of bran and endosperm is required. Milling of whole wheat flour, may therefore be accomplished by simply using a stonemill or hammermill. However, where a special flour is required i.e. with a special granulation. Ash content or colour grade, than a number of complex machines are needed.

Cleaning and conditioning

Before being stored in silos, the wheat is given a preliminary cleaning in order to protect the machinery and to improve the storage conditions. Accurate and adjustable grain scales discharge the wheat from the silo bins so that the required blend is obtained.

A number of cleaning machines remove all foreign seeds and impurities such as sand, stones, weed seeds, dust etc. To improve the milling conditions a small amount of water is added to toughen the bran and mellow the endosperm. Scourers clean the surface of the wheat before the grinding process is begun.

Principles of milling

The endosperm and bran are tightly bound together. Therefore to ensure that the endosperm is not damaged and as little is wasted as possible the grain must be broken down carefully.

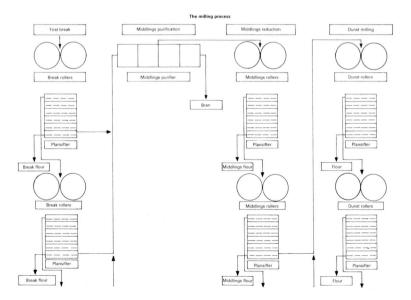

Break system

The purpose of the break rollers is to break open the wheat kernel and to scrape off the endosperm from the bran. This is generally done in 4 or 5 steps so as to produce small endosperm particles and coarse bran with minimum production of bran powder. Through careful grinding on each break, minimal cutting of the bran takes place and the subsequent separation in the sifters is more efficient. The surfaces of the break rolls are fluted (grooved) and the two rollers turn at different r.p.m.

Purification

Even with the best conditioning and the most carefully set breaking system some of the bran will be cut into small particles having the same size as semolina or middlings. To remove these bran particles from the semolina and middlings, purifiers are used. These cleaning machines are based on the separation by specific weight. A constant air stream through a sieve causes the lighter bran particles to float, they fly upwards and are caught in fine break rollers. The heavier semolina and middling particles fall through the sieve and are fed into the first reduction rollers.

Reduction

Clean semolina and middlings from the purification system are gradually reduced by smooth rollers into flour particles. Each reduction passage is followed by a sieving process, the remains being set aside for blending. Depending on the hardness of the semolina up to 12 reductions may be necessary.

Flour composition

The various flours from the different passages are blended together to produce the desired flours required.

Flour yield

Approximately 82% of the wheat kernel is endosperm and 18% is bran and germ. Pure endosperm from the centre of the kernel has an ash content of about 0.35% where as the ash content of the bran is as high as 5%. The ash content of a flour is therefore an indication as to how well the bran has been separated in the milling process i.e. the pureness of the flour. The higher the ash content the higher the amount of bran present. This in turn bears a relationship to the flour yield. The percentage flour yield, indicates how much flour was extracted from the wheat kernel.

Main flour types in Switzerland

Type	Yield	Composition
Whole wheat flour Type 1900	98%	Apart from the top skinlayer and some germ it contains all parts of the kernel.
Dark flour Type 1100	80—85%	62% dark flour and 20% white flour which has been removed.
Half white flour Type 720	72—75%	56% half white flour and 20% white flour which has been remouved.
White flour Type 550	60—65%	straight run flour
White flour Type 400	20—30%	produced simultaneously with dark or half white flour.

Schematic breakdown showing yields of various milled products

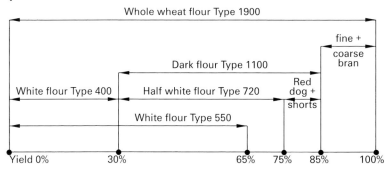

The internationally used chemical and physical dough tests together with a baking test from the basis for the assessment of baking quality.

The flour quality

Because of the wide range of recipes and the different processing methods in the baking trade, a so called "all purpose flour" is mainly used. In order to maintain or even improve the high standard of baked products, this flour has to be of top quality.

Quality specification

With the help of standardized testing methods the properties of the flour and the dough can be analized. When evaluating the test results, one has to consider the relationships involved. Very often it is necessary to carry out a test bake in order to get a final idea of the baking quality of the flour.

Protein/gluten complex

The protein quantity of a flour can be analized by the protein test. The sedimentation test or Zeleny test indicates the protein quality. The water insoluble proteins, the so called gluten, are of great importance for gas retention and the development of the dough during the baking process. The gluten quantity is analized by the gluten test whereas the gluten quality is analised by the swelling number test. The water absorbtion is measured using the Farinograph. The shape and size of the curve gives some indication of the dough properties such as development and dough stability. With the help of the Extensograph dough extensibility and dough resistance is measured. The ratio of these two figures is also an indicator of the dough characteristics. The area covered by the extensogramm curve is a guide to the bread volume to be expected.

Starch complex

The gelatinization properies of the starch are measured with the amylograph or viskograph, they give a good indication of the crumb formation during baking and of the crumb texture of the final product. The starch properties also influence the water retention capicity during dough formation (they can be damaged to some extent during the milling process). The maltose production capacity of the flour influences the rising ability of the dough in that the maltose is formed from degraded starch and serves directly as yeast food. Moreover the browning reaction is enhanced in the presence of sugars.

Enzyme complex

Apart from the "falling number", which can be regarded as a method for the determination of amounts of alpha-amylase, the effect of starch degrading enzymes can also be obtained indirectly, be it with the liquefacation number of the amylogram or with the ratio between pre-existing sugars and the maltose production capacity. The proteolytic activity is shown in the softening of the faringram curve and in the reduction of the swelling number, although the results vary according to the gluten quantity and quality.

Baking Tests

The chemical and physical tests evaluate the different quality factors individually, whereas in the baking test the interactions between protein/gluten, starch and enzymes are evaluated and allow a final estimation of the quality of a flour. It is a basic requirement however that the test conditions are exactly laid down and standardized. Other factors such as yeast quality and working methods may still have considerable influence on the final result. The baking test can give an indication of flour quality only under the preset test conditions. Therefore it is often necessary to use several different baking tests, as is done for example when assessing the baking quality of new wheat varieties. The methods used in Switzerland for this purpose will be briefly described in the following.

Rapid-Mix-Test

Standard method of the "Arbeitsgemeinschaft Getreideforschung Detmold" for a flour type 550.
The baking test (with bread-rolls) is based on a dough consistency of 500 Brabender Units (BU). The flours are adjusted to a falling number of 250 with malt flour and ascorbic acid (2 ppm) being added. The recipe prescribes also the addition of fat and sugar. After a very intensive mixing (mixer at 1400 rpm) rolls are prepared in a moulding machine.
Crumb and crust properties as well as bread volume are measured and graded.

Blend baking test

Standard method of Dr. W. Saurer, Swiss Federal Research Station for Agronomy, Zurich-Reckenholz. The working method is the same as the Rapid-Mix-Test. The variety to be tested is blended 1:1 with a commercial bakery flour, and the blending value is calculated from the differences in bread volume.

Tin baking test

Standard method of the Swiss School of Baking, Richemont, Lucerne, for all types of flours.
The baking test with tin baked bread is based on a dough consistency of 360 BU. Contrary to the Rapid-Mix-Test the mixing is done with much less intensity (Diosna laboratory mixer, 120 rpm). There is no addition of malt, ascorbic acid, sugar or fat.
After an initial proof of 2 hrs the dough is divided and left for final proof of

60 — 75 — 90 minutes for white flour
45 — 60 — 75 minutes for half-white flours
30 — 45 — 60 minutes for dark flours

This way we can determine the optimal final proof time. The moulding of the dough is done manually.

CIBM baking test

Standard baking test of the Swiss School of Baking, Richemont, elaborated in cooperation with the Centre professionnel des Boulangers romands, (CIBM), Pully. This test is applied at the wheat variety testing stage.
In accordance with the bread type usually produced in the western part of Switzerland doughs are prepared from 5 to 10 kg of flour type 550 and based on a dough consistency of 360 BU. After an initial proof of 2.5 hrs the dough is devided and moulded mechanically to give a bread with a weight of 500 g. The dough pieces are placed directly on a loading apparatus and left for 50 min for final proof. Evaluation of the bread volume and the bread characteristics is done according to the official scheme for bread quality rating by the Swiss School of Baking, Richemont, Lucerne.

Large scale baking test

Is the standard baking test used in the Richemont Craft School for new wheat varieties form the milling and baking trials by the Federal Department of Agriculture. 1 kg bread loaves are produced from half-white and dark flours. The working methods closely follow the normal procedures in the bakery. For big loaves either a long straighth-dough method with a fermentation time of 8 hrs or a short straight-dough process with an initial proof of 70 min is used. In order to get some indications of the stress tolerance of the doughs the moulding is done mechanically and the dough pieces are placed directly on a loading apparatus. The evaluation of the baked goods is done in the same way as in the CIBM baking test.

Characteristics of Commercial Baking Flours

The average value for unheated flours with no addition of ascorbic acid, malt flour, dry gluten, pre-gelatinized flour, lecithin, enzyme compounds.

Testing methods		Flour strength			
		White wheat flour Type 400	White wheat flour Type 550	Half-white wheat flour Type 720	Dark wheat flour Type 1100
Ash content % (dry matter)	min.		0,49	0,64	1,00
	max.	0,48	0,58	0,76	1,15
moisture content %	basic value	14,0	14,0	14,0	14,0
Protein content % (TS, N × 5,7)	min.	11,5	12,0	12,5	13,0
Zeleny Sedimentation value	min.	45	40	38	30
Gluten, wet %	min.	27	27	28	29
Water absorption % 500 BE	min.	59	60	61	64
360 BE	min.	64	65	66	69
Extensogram ratio (R/E)		2–3	2–3	1,5–2,5	1,5–2,5
area cm^2 (135')	min.	120	110	100	80
Amylogram Viscosity BE (Mid value)		600	600	400	300
Falling number	min.	330	330	310	300
Maltose %	max.	2,3	2,3	2,4	2,5
Baking test Volume from 100 g of flour ml.	min.	550	520	500	480

Special Purpose Flours

White flour, type 550

This flour type (straight-run flour) is used mainly by industrial bakeries. According to the higher extraction rate compared to a conventional white flour this flour shows a weaker gluten quality and a higher enzymatic activity. Type 550 was created as a substitute for white flour. It can be used for baked goods which have no high demands on dough stability, loaf volume or crumb colour. In a craft bakery often 1/3 of the white flour is replaced by half-white flour instead of using a type 550 flour.

Graham flour

Graham flour is the most commonly used type of wholemeal, and is used in different amounts and different granulations (fine, medium, coarse) for different speciality breads. According to the Swiss allotment of cereals to the mills, Graham flour is usually not a pure wheat product but contains up to 7% rye.

Chop flours

Chop flours from wheat and rye are offered in different granulations, mainly as wholemeal, and are used for various dark speciality breads.
Chop flours with special methods of preparation (Dr. Bircher, Steinmetz, Duro) have to be produced according to official regulations.

Rye flours

Rye is used as a special purpose flour, it is available as a half-white and dark flour as well as a coarse whole meal, with a fine, medium or coarse granulation.

Flour blends

The most important flour blend is the "Farmer's flour" (70–80% wheat, 20–30% rye) which comes as half-white or dark type on the market. Farmer's Special flour contains 2% of acidulated skimmed milk powder. There are many other types of blends but their popularity usually remains regional. Many blends for special breads are prepared in the bakeries themselves from commercially available flours. Rye bread may by law contain no more than 1/3 of wheat flour which improves the bread's baking characteristics.

Dark wheat flours

The consumer's wish for highly nutritional dark breads has also been taken into consideration with large loaves. Apart from the usual dark flour types available, many darker flours have been brought onto the market. In order not to impair the baking quality too much, selected passages of shorts and millstreams, rich in bran, are included in the flour blends.

Baker's yeast

Yeast in the past and today

During his daily handling of yeast, the professional seldom realises that the yeast in today's form only exists since the beginning of this century.

For more than 6000 years doughs were more or less unknowingly aerated by wild yeasts. Not until 1680 did von Leeuwenhoek first observe the yeast as a microorganism under the microscope. The exact proof, that the alcoholic fermentation was connected with the activity of the yeast, was only discovered in the middle of the 19th. Centuary. Baker's yeast was produced by the breweries. First of all, surface fermented yeast, and afterwards submerged fermented yeast was used for the preparation of bread, where from the multifarious strains of the genus sacchoromyces cerevisiae were selected and bred. They form the basis of today's baker's yeast.

In Switzerland yeast is produced in the three factories, namely Hindelbank, Klipfel Rheinfelden and Stettfurt. It is a standard yeast with good saccharose- and maltose fermentation properties. Yeasts with 20—30% higher or quicker activity are not made in Switzerland.

Yeast production

Yeast production

One single cell from the mother yeast is put under conditions of high aeration, together with molasses and other nutrients such as phosphate and nitrogen. Absolute cleanless is necessary in order to avoid any infections. In addition, great experience is needed to be able to create optimal conditions for the growing of the yeast. Under steady observation and control the harvested yeast creme is washed and filtered to a water content of 70—75%. It should then have a uniform drive activity.

Fresh yeast has a light ivory color and has a shell shaped structure when broken.

1. Molasses
2. Water
3. Ammonia
4. Phosphate
5. Heat exchanger
6. Pure strain
7. Pure reproduced Mother yeast
8. Air

9. Fermentation Vat
10. Deaeration
11. Cooling water
12. Centrifuge
13. Cooling
14. Waste water treatment
15. Yeast cream
16. Rotary filter
17. Packing

Yeast reproduction during dough development

A strong heathly yeast must be used to aerate a long-straight dough, because little yeast is added and it is important that the yeast reproduces well. When little yeast is added (10–20 g per liter) and enough time is given (8–10 hours) the yeast is able to reproduce itself doubly. When the dough contains more than 2% yeast the bulk fermentation time is greatly reduced, and almost no yeast reproduction takes place. The art of controlling the dough development lies in handling the yeast as a living organism.

Yeast reproduction

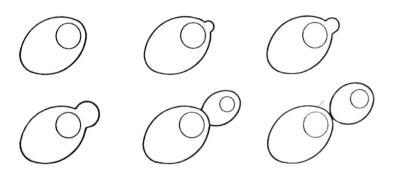

At first a small swelling occurs on one side of the yeast cell. This continues to enlargen and eventually it achieves the size of a yeast cell. As soon as this daughter cell reaches a certain size it will split off from the mother cell. The new cell is fully developed and is immediately capable of living alone.

Storing yeast correctly

Yeast, being an unicellular sprout-fungy with the size of a thousandth of a millimeter, is very sensitive to temperature changes. The yeast – 1 gram of yeast cotains about 10 milliards single cells – must be able to breath during storage. In comparison to fermentation about 3–4 times more energy is used during storage. When the storage temperature is raised the rate of breathing becomes more intense, and it is possible that yeast cell breaks down its own protein causing the cell to die. Baker's yeast must be stored in a cool place i. e. at a temperature of 4–8 °C in the fridge. Partly used yeast must not be left long in the warm bakery otherwise differences in the rising power occur.
Correctly stored baker's yeast, even when it is slightly dry and crumbly, will still have sufficient rising power for a short direct fermentation process.
There is always plenty of discussion on the subject of deep freezing yeast.
If we consider the structure of the yeast cell, the cell protoplasma, the cell centre and the fine membrane it is easy to understand that freezing will have an effect on the living functions of the cell. However, because the fermentation process depends on the enzymes contained in the yeast and not on any of it's living functions, it is possible to achieve sufficient dough aeration, even with frozen yeast, which is, therefore partly damaged. The ability of the yeast to reproduce is also reduced. This can have an effect on doughs containing little yeast, because during the long fermentation time no reproduction takes place. Thus yeast can be frozen and still be able to areate doughs but it loses some of its reproduction abilities. During storage the aerating power of the yeast decreases. It should not be stored longer than 6 months. It is important that the yeast is frozen correctly and is not stored for a long time otherwise the yeast will partly liquify on thawing-out. Frozen yeast should be left to thaw-out in the fridge, not at room temperature.

Dry yeast

In order to preserve fresh yeast it is possible to carefully withdraw water from it. Dry yeast has a water content of 4–6%. It is advantageous to store it in airtight bags, in a cool, dry place. Once the bag is opened it must be used quickly. In Switzerland dry yeast is almost only used in the household. The quantity of dry yeast to be used is about 1/4–1/3 of the quantity of fresh yeast. Active dry yeast can be added directly to the flour. However normal dry yeast should be dissolved in water at 40–45° C and a little sugar should be added to activate it.

Sour Dough

General

This process is the oldest form of bread production. Is was even known to the ancient egyptians. Due to the activity of certain lactic acid bacertia and special yeasts the dough begins to ferment and becomes sour. This process can be regulated by controlling the firmness of the dough, the temperature and the bulk fermentation time. Sour dough bread stays fresh for a long time and has a particularly
strong flavour. With doughs containing a lot of rye flour the baking and swelling behaviour is improved due to the development of acids. To make sour dough it requires a very careful method of production and a lot of experience. Even though acid bread requires more time and skill to produce it is still becoming more and more popular with the customers. This is due to its stronger flavour and its freshness.

Making sour dough

The sour dough is developed by leaving the dough to stand for a long time and allowing the wild yeasts to multiply. If a piece of ripe sour dough is already available this can be used to develop the new dough. There are also many sour dough starters on the market which contain the micro-organisms found in sour dough. In the initial stages of developing a sour dough it is advantageous to use flours with a high extraction rate (e.g. dark rye flour or dark flour). This is because they contain more enzymes and more simple sugars, which help the fermentation process. On the otherhand flour from sprouted grain has a negative effect on the development of sour dough.

Developing sour dough

By controlling the dough development one can regulate the lactic acid development (warm and moist) and the acetic acid development (cool and firm). The ripe sour dough should contain lactic and acetic acids in the relationship of 75:25 to 80:20. If the acetic acid content is too high then the acidic taste is too strong. If the lactic acid content is to high then the taste is dull and tasteless.

Sour dough yeasts

Depending on the fermentation process and the development of acids, certain yeasts are able to assert themselves. There are many types of yeasts, each with their own properties. Thus apart from normal sour dough yeasts, which can tolerate high acidity and have good fermentation properties, other taste developing yeasts are also present.

Faults in making sour dough

Due to incorrect dough development or over-ripe or under-ripe sour dough, it is possible for microorganisms to assert themselves causing bad taste and bad bread quality. If such a dough is continually used as a starter for fresh sour dough, then it is possible for germs, bacillus and unwanted yeasts to develop.

Making the sour dough starter

The Swiss method of making sour dough takes five days before a fermentable starter is produced. This is then used to round off the taste of bread and other bakery products containing a high percentage of wheat flour. It is used together with a normal sponge or ferment (50–100 g per liter). It can also be used to improve the baking properties of rye flour doughs (100–200 g per liter). When storing the starter in a cool place it is important not to let it become too sour. This is done by refreshing it every 2 days with an amount of water equal to its weight and double its weight of flour. If should then be left at room temperature for 1–2 hours before being stored away again.

Sour dough sponge for daily or weekly production

Water, 40°C	1000 g	1000 g	1000 g	1000 g
Levit-Fermenta, active* (sour dough starter)	200 g	200 g	200 g	200 g
Dark wheat flour, Type 1100	1800 g			
Half-white wheat flour, Typ 720		1800 g		
Whole wheat flour, Type 1900			1500 g	
Dark rye flour Type 1100				1200 g

Carfully knead the ingredients. Place sour dough sponge in a plastic jar and store for *24 hours at 35° C.*

After the developing phase can the sour dough sponge be worked or placed in the refrigerator for a week without quality loss.

The sour dough sponge can be used for big breads, special breads as well as small articles.

* Levit-Fermenta, active

Ingredients:
Dried sour dough from fermented wheat and rye flours, enzymes (Amylasen).

Bread Improvers

Origins and effects of

Because of their origins, different bread improvers have different effects on a dough. Bread improvers with a natural origin (eg. malt) are called "ingredients" and those produced on a chemical basis (eg. emulsifiers) are known as "additives". Only the baker can decide how much he can afford to satisfy the increasing demands for more natural products.
It is best to categorise the bread improvers according to their effects.

Legislation

There are strict laws in Switzerland concerning the use and declaration of additives. Those additives allowed are named and listed.

The use in Large Breads

Lecithin being a natural ingredient, is the only type of emulsifier allowed. It is won in great quantities from the soja plant. Lecithin is also contained in the egg and the wheat germ where it is found dissolved in fat. Other natural bread improvers are citric acid, lactic acid, tartaric acid and their derivative salts. These natural metabolic products are produced in small quantities during the ripening of the dough. The enzymes amylase and protease cause the dough to ripen. Depending on the harvest, occasionally not enough enzymes are contained in the grain. They then have to be added to the flour as an enzyme preparation. Vitamin C (ascorbic acid) found in many

The use of

Bread improvers can generally be defined as products which are added to a dough to improve its' baking properties, to improve the quality of the finished product, or to prevent product fluctuations and simplify production. The raw materials, the work process and the finished product must all be taken into consideration before the choice of bread improvers is made.

LMV chapter	Food product	LMV article	Additives	Maximum amounts	Declaration for pre-packed foods	Effects
12.1	Bread	142	Emulsifiers: Lecithin	GPP*	Emulsifier	
			Alkalis, acids, salts:	GPP	Individual	
			citric acid, acetic acid, latic acid,		descripton or	Inhibits the
			tartaric acid and their derivative salts		flavouring acids	development
						of rope
			Enzyme compounds: amylase, protease	GPP	No declaration	
			Other additives: ascorbic acid (vitamin C)	GPP	Dough conditoner	Gluten tightening
12.2	Special breads, fermented small goods	143, 144	Preservatives: propionic acid	3 g/kg Flour	Individual description	
			Emulsifiers: Lecithin	GPP	Emulsifier	
			Mono- and diglycerids of fatty acids, as well as esters of mono- and di-glycerides of fatty acids, sugar esters and sugar glycerides.	10 g/kg		
			Sodium-potassium-calcium lactylate	5 g/kg Flour		
			Alkalis, acids, salts:	GPP	Individual description	
			citric acid, acetic acid, latic acid,		or flavouring	
			tartaric acid and their derivative salts		acids	
			certain chlorides and carbonates	1 g/kg		
			phosphates and sulphates		Dough conditioner	
			Enzyme compounds: amylase, protease Pentosanase, invertase	GPP	No declaration	
			Other additives: ascorbic acid (vitamin C)	GPP	Dough conditioner	Gluten tightening

LMV = Lebensmittelverordnung i. e. Book of laws concerning food products
*GPP = **G**ood **P**roduction **P**ractice i.e. as much as is necessary to achieve the desired result.

fruits, can cause the tightening of the gluten, even in very small amounts (1—2 g per 100 kg flour).

The use in special breads and small goods

No artificial emulsifiers are allowed to be used in special breads and small goods. Only in the case of pre-packed special breads is the use of modified emulsifiers (unnatural additives) allowed, these being certain phosphates and pure propionic acid.

Effects of bread improvers

Type of bread improver	Origin	Forms available	Use	Bakery products	Effects
1. Malt products					
1.1. To improve panary fermentation	Made from dried, sprouted barley or wheat	Malt extract, dry malt extract, malt flour	For light flours with low enzyme quantities	White bread, fermented small goods	As malt sugar can be directly assimilated by yeast, it aids the fermentation of a dough, making it more elastic and pliable. It aids the browing and hinders the crumb from drying out
1.2. To improve the development of the taste and improve the bread compostion	As 1.1., enriched with yeast foods and easily assimilated sugars	Powdered form	To correct fluctuations in the flour quality brought on by the harvest	Additive for bread and special breads	As 1.1., Aids natural food conversion during fermentation
1.3. To prevent product fluctuations and simplify production	As 1.1 and 1.2 combined with natural proving agents	liquid ferment dry ferment	To correct fluctuations in proving conditions To balance variations in the raw materials	Mainly for bread and special breads	stabilises the proving process
1.4. Gluten tightening products	Ascorbic acid-starch mixtures (vitamin C)	Powdered form	For doughs made from weak flours. For doughs with very long proving times (extended proving, interrupted proving) For doughs to be moulded by machine	large bread fermented small goods	Tightens the gluten. Stabilizes the dough, prevents wide flowing doughs
1.5. Enzyme compounds	Pure compounds isolated from plant life or micro-organisms and bound together with a carrier substance (starch)	Powdered form	For laminated yeast doughs	Croissants	Breaks down starch and protein, lessens the dependance on proving time
2. Products containing emulsifiers	Combinations of fats emulsifiers and easily assimilated sugar	Pastes. powdered form	To aid the binding of the dough and thus improve it's gas containing ability	Small breads and special breads containing fats or milk. The use of emulsifiers is prohibited for large breads	Lessens dependance on proving time, makes the crumb structure finer, the crust more delicate and the volume larger
3. Preservatives	Products made on the basis of propionic acid	Pure compounds often mixed with carrier substances to ease dosage	Inhibits the development of mould	For prepacked special breads and flour confectionery	Inhibits the growth of damaging micro-organisms
	Salts derived from acetic acid		Inhibits the development of rope	Used for some large breads	

The Nutritional value of bread

People's eating habits have changed greatly over the last ten years. Today more meat and sugar products are consumed and less cereal and potatoe products. Because bread is such a balanced nutrient it is still seen as an important basic foodstuff. No other foodstuff can claim to be consumed daily, in so many forms, and still remain popular. In 1980, in Basel, a survey was carried out by professor Ritzel. Of the people asked 45% regarded bread as the most important foodstuff available.

	Wholemeal Bread	Dark Bread	Semi White
Nutritional Value (per 100 g)			
Water	37,1 g	35,0 g	33,0 g
Carbohydrates	44,0 g	50,6 g	54,3 g
Protein	9,0 g	8,2 g	7,6 g
Fat	1,5 g	1,2 g	1,0 g
Dietary Fibres	6,2 g	2,7 g	1,9 g
Energy	225 kcal	246 kcal	257 kcal
	943 kJ	1028 kJ	1074 kJ
Mineral salts			
Iron	2,6 mg	1,7 mg	1,1 mg
Sodium	625,0 mg	708,0 mg	739,0 mg
Potassium	240,0 mg	168,0 mg	128,0 mg
Calcium	62,4 mg	39.0 mg	30,8 mg
Magnesium	68,1 mg	40,9 mg	25,8 mg
Phosphorus	196,0 mg	147,0 mg	108,0 mg
Vitamins			
Thiamine (B$_1$)	0,222 mg	0,202 mg	0,099 mg
Riboflavin (B$_2$)	0,094 mg	0,079 mg	0,052 mg
Niacin	1.970 mg	1,346 mg	0,870 mg

The nutritional contribution to persons's daily requirements of 200 g wholemeal bread

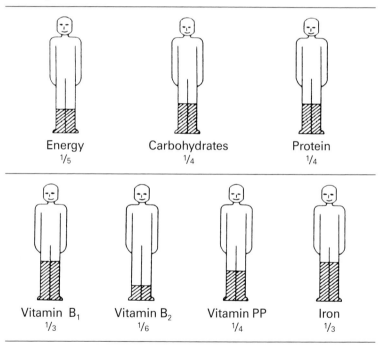

Energy	Carbohydrates	Protein
1/5	1/4	1/4

Vitamin B$_1$	Vitamin B$_2$	Vitamin PP	Iron
1/3	1/6	1/4	1/3

Thanks to its balanced compostion, bread is the most important basic foodstuff. With his wide range of products the baker provides the foundation for a good, heathly diet.

Bread consumption

According to the BIGA statistics, bread consumption today is approximately 28 kg per person per annum. This means a daily intake of 75 g.
However, these figures do not include bread eaten outside the home. This mainly concerns the consumption of small bread and small articles and raises the daily consumption figures to 130–150 g per person.

Bread consumption at the different mealtimes

Mealtime	%										
Breakfast	78%	■	■	■	■	■	■	■	◧	□	□
Nine O'clock	29%	■	■	■	□	□	□	□	□	□	□
Midday meal	36%	■	■	■	◧	□	□	□	□	□	□
Four O'clock	24%	■	■	◧	□	□	□	□	□	□	□
Evening meal	74%	■	■	■	■	■	■	■	◧	□	□

Breakfast and the evening meal are clearly the two most popular times for eating bread. It is surprising that considering the popularity of bread and other bakery products relatively little is eaten inbetween meal times.

The Nutrional value of bread

Nutrients are unevenly dispersed throughout the cereal grain. The centre of the grain, the endospern, contains mainly carbohydrates, where-as the bran coatings contain most of the nutritionally valuable proteins. Minerals and vitamins are also contained in the bran coatings as well as in the germ (iron, vitamin E). The outer coatings of the grain are made up of cellulose (long chains of carbohydrates). These dietary fibres cannot be digested by the human body but still play an important part in the digestive system as roughage (saliva, time spent in the stomache, bowelmovements, faeces composition). For a long time the functions of dietary fibres were unappreciated (trend towards refined foodstuffs). Only recently has the consumption of sufficient dietary fibres become popular (30–35 g per day).
Because of the varied composition of the different parts of the grain, the nutritional values of a bread depend on the extraction rate of the flour used. In making a good nutritious bread, one must take into consideration people's eating habits and the increasing public awareness of nutritional values. The bread should have:
— low food energy content
  (reduced carbohydrates and fat)
— high nutritional values i.e.
  — rich in nutritionally valuable proteins
  — rich in vitamins of the B complex
  — rich in minerals, especially iron
— high dietary fibre content

Bread and Baking Consumption 1987–1992
At home and outside food supply (gram per person/day):

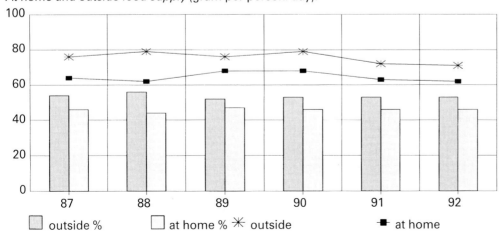

outside % | at home % | ✳ outside | ■ at home

The outside consumption of **71,5 g** per person/day (53,5%) still exceeds the home consumption 62,5 g (46,5%).

The bread assortment in the bakery

In Switzerland over a hundred different types of bread are produced, as well as more than a hundred different small breads and small articles. It is the bakers' task to produce the most popular breads and goods from this assortment, so as to be able to sell as much as possible, The basic, balanced assortment of products ranges from white to dark and wholemeal breads as well, as many well known special breads. Through the bakers associations' special offers and his own creations, the baker is always able to offer new and interesting alternatives, where-by great emphasis is laid upon the healthy, nutritious value of each new bread.

According to the Swiss food regulations, the wide ranging assortment of bread and bakery products can be devided into the following categories:

Bakery products

Large bread
Special bread
Small bread
Small articles
Zopf goods

The category-bakery products concerns all water breads as well as all breads and products containing milk, butter, and eggs. The division into large bread, special bread, small bread, small articles and zopf goods is also used in compiling statistics concerning people's eating habits.

Large bread

Produced with pure baking flours (half-white or dark flour). Breads may only be sold with a weight of 250, 500, 1000, 1500 and 2000 g.

Dark bread

Also known as "black" bread. The flour's high extraction rate causes the bread to have a stronger taste and to stay fresh longer.

Half-white bread

Also known as "light" bread. Has a mild but aromatic taste, and does not stay fresh long.

Canton breads

The bread types produced in the different cantons can generally be made from both dark and half-white flour. Compared to normal long and round bread, the production methods are different (dough consistency, dough conditioning, moulding, baking process) and therefore so too is the bread's form, appearance, crust and crumb texture, and taste. It is left to the individual cantons to determin the acceptable water content of their particular bread, in general the limit is 40–42%.

Special breads

Special breads are produced from flours of different extraction rates (white, half-white, dark and wholemeal flour) and from different cereals (wheat, rye, mixtures of several cereals). They may be sold at any weight over 150 g.

Wholemeal bread

Made only from wholemeal flours containing the complete grain. These flours have an extraction rate of 98%. The addition of other flours to improve the baking qualities is forbidden.

Rye bread

Of the total flour content, two thirds must be rye flour. Light and dark rye flours are used as well as soured coarse whole rye meal.

Other special breads

By taking the main type of flour used for a bread (white, half-white, dark and wholemeal flour) it is possible to categorize the bread types. Those special breads which are enriched with nutritonally valuable ingredients are subject to strict regulations. Only a restricted amount may be added to a dough so that the bread still retains its typical characteristics.

Flans, tarts and pizzas

Products made from different doughs. Filled with fuits, vegetables, cheese etc. with or without topping.

Characteristics:	Typical products:
— Sweet tarts:	
Products with sweet toppings and eventually other addition	Fresh cream tarts Nut tarts
Products covered with fruits and with addition of more or less sweet topping	Addition of apples, apricots, plums, cherries, rhubarb
Fruit tarts without topping	Same addition of fruits
— Salted tarts:	
Products with salted cheese topping	Cheese tarts
Products with salted cheese topping or other ingredients	cheese and tomatoe tarts, Cheese an oignons tarts, Quiche Lorraine, Cheese and mushruoom tarts
Products with vegetables or salted toppings	Spinach an bacon tarts, Ratatouille, Potatoe and bacon tarts
— Pizzas:	
Special dough garnished with tomatoes, melted cheese, ham, anchovies, pepper, olives and different spices	Pizza à la mode du chef, Pizza Napolitana, Pizza Quattro Stagione

Large bread Dark and Half white flour	Special bread Whole wheat flour	Special bread White flour	Special bread Half white flour	Special bread mostly dark flour types with additives	Special bread Diatetic bread
Aargau bread	Whole wheat bread	Parisette	Bürli bread	Rustico bread	Colic bread
Appenzell-/	Graham bread	Paris bread	Tessin bread	Gupf bread	Diabetic bread
Thurgau bread	Duro bread	– Baguettes	Biopan	Yoghurt bread	Glutenbread
Basel bread	Dr. Bircher bread	– Flûtes	Filoncino	Rome bread	Diabetic wheat-germ
Bern bread	Steinmetz bread	– Ficelles		Granary bread	bread
Freiburg bread	Vitalin bread	Pain fleur		Fruit bread	Diabetic whole wheat
Genf bread	Kernen bread	Schilt bread		Nut bread	bread
Glarus bread	Schrot bread	Toast bread		Pear bread	Diabetic nut bread
Jura bread	Nature bread	Milk bread		Wheat flake bread	Salt-free bread
Luzern bread	Ariana bread	Sunday bread		Wheat germ bread	(Sodium free)
Neuenburg bread	Three corn bread	Model bread		Maize bread	Low salt bread
Nidwalden bread	Four corn bread	Pane reale		Oatmeal bread	(Low sodium)
Obwalden bread	Five corn bread	Cornetti bread		Barley bread	Diet soya
St. Gallen bread	Five corn bread	Mailand bread		Potato bread	
Schaffhausen bread	(with baking powder)	Pane nostrano		Bran bread	
(Commis bread)	Six corn bread	Ciampa Locarnese		Linseed bread	
Solothurn bread	Wallis bread	(Four finger bread)		Sesame bread	
Schwyz-/Zug bread	Rye grain bread	Micca		Soya bread	
Uri bread	Pumpernickel	Pane Biove		Poppyseed bread	
Waadtland Cross-bread		Pain d'épi		Malt bread	
– Weggen		Pain de la Champagne		Sour dough bread	
– Carrelé				Vallemaggia	
Zürich bread				Rye ring bread	
				Rye carraway bread	
				Rye nut bread	
				Brasciadela	
				Farmer bread	
				Farmer bread with fresh milk	
				Farmer rye bread	
				Party bread	

Small pieces

Products made from different doughs such as buttered sweet dough and various masses: biscuit mass, butter mass, meringue, macaroon mass, combined with jam, candied or dried fruits or with nuts.

Characteristics: Not filled with cream, but combined with jam, candied or dried fruits or nuts.

Typical products: Sablés, vanilla brezel, almond or hazelnut sticks, butter-S, madelaines, macaroons, bird's nest, amaretti, chocolate-S, coconut macaroon and puff paste articles

Gingerbread and beavers

Mostly prepared from honey doughs, unfilled or filled or by using enriched products, sold as big pieces, small pieces or petits fours. Exception: The Lucerne honey cake which is made with concentrated pear juice.

Characteristics:
— Unfilled with royal icing, pressed paper pictures or marzipan.
— Filled with almond or hazelnut filling mostly pressed in moulds.
— Enriched with orange, lemon peels, chopped almonds.
— The soda taste is typical for the Lucerne honey cake.

Typical products: Gingerbreads, fladen, beavers, basler tit-bits, hazelnut honey cake, magen bread (fair), small honey nuts, Lucerne honey cake

Deep fried articles

Under this label, one understands that the products are not baked but fried eiher in fat or oil. Most of these articles are sold on certain occasions (i.e. carnival, annual fairs) and individually.

Characteristics: As filling, one uses jam, curd cheese, almond mass, pear bread filling, vanilla cream, sultanas or candied fruits. The products are mostly dusted with icing sugar or cinnamon sugar.

Typical products: Berliner (Doughnuts), Schluferli, little thighs, carnival cakes, stork's nest, Zurich and Central Switzerland Zigerkrapfen, little rose cakes, Ziger balls and piped choux pastries.

Dietetic bread

Bread which due to its compostion fulfills the nutritional needs of people requiring special foods (Diabetics, low sodium content, sodium free, gluten free) is subject to strict regulations. (Article 180–185 of the LMV). In particular the regulations concern the breads' careful production, the wrapping and the declaration on the packing (nutritional content, producer, date). In order to be able to sell such a product one must have the approval of the federal health department. Grants are only given after a detailed laboratory analysis of the product to be sold.

Bread for diabetics

In comparison to normal bread, this must contain a considerably reduced quantity of carbohydrates (usually one-third less). Apart from stating the nutritional values of the carbohydrates, protein, fats and water contained, one must declare the bread value (corresponding to 10 g of carbohydrates) or the bread unit (corresponding to 12,5 g of carbohydrates). This enables the diabetic to calculate his eating rations.

Saltless bread

Only bread containing less than 0.1% sodium may be declared salt reduced or sodium reduced. To be called saltless or sodiumless it must contain less than 0.02% Sodium. If dietsalt is used to enhance the flavour, it must be ensured that its composition complies with the patients requirements.

Gluten-free bread

Colitis is an illness concerning the inflamation of the intestines which occurs mainly amongst small children. Because the intestines react strongly against gliadin (a part of gluten) a very strict diet is required. In the production of a suitable bread, no wheat, rye, barley or oat flour may be used. It is only possible to produce such a bread using soya and milk protein (available as a flour) and starch.

The bread

It is the aim of every Master Baker to produce a bread of outstanding quality. That is well aerated, is tasty and has an appetizing appearance. The decisive factors in the production of such a bread are flour quality, dough mixing, dough temperature, dough fermentation, dough manipulation, dough moulding, proving and baking.

Guide lines for the production of large breads, small breads and special breads

General

The choice of products the baker has to offer is almost equal to the choice of methods available to him in the production of his goods. Each method has its' advantages and disadvantages. In order to succeed, each step must correspond with the next. The following guidelines are therefore only basic. It still requires the indepth skills of a craftsman to control the dough processing, the dough fermentation, the moulding and the baking of the bread. Only then can the baker be sure to produce a bread of high quality.

The breadmaking process

The correct choice of breadmaking process depends greatly upon the ingredients and upon the characteristics of the product being made. The baker must decide which breadmaking process suits his needs best. He does this according to his business structure, his production programm and his personal efforts to produce a product of high quality.

The indirect breadmaking process

The indirect breadmaking process concerns the step by step production of a dough. A primary dough is produced which is later added to the main dough. The primary dough or ferment has the following functions:
— It allows the gluten time to swell and absorb water
— The yeast quantity multiplies by 30% during eight hours of fermentation
— Development of bread aroma

— Development of lactic and acetic acids which keep the bread fresh and influence the development of the characteristic bread aroma.
There are four indirect breadmaking process:
— the overnight sponge and dough process (8—10 hours)
— the short sponge and dough process (2—4 hours)
— the quick ferment
— the pouliche
Each method has its' advantages and is particularly suitable for the production of certain products.

The overnight sponge and dough process

Suitable for large bread, special breads and simple small bread varieties.

Fermentation time:	8—10 hours
Sponge fraction:	$1/4$—$1/3$ of the main dough
Yeast quantity:	10—30 g per liter of fluids, of which $1/5$ is added to the sponge
Sponge temperature:	16—20° C
Sponge consistency:	same as main dough
Sponge ripeness:	the sponge should collapse slightly but be allowed to rise again

The short sponge and dough process

Suitable for special breads, small articles and yeast pastries

Fermentation time:	2—4 hours
Sponge fraction:	approximately $1/2$ of the main dough
Yeast quantity:	30—40 g per liter of fluids. According to the fermentation time an additional 20—40 g per liter of fluids may be added
Sponge temperature:	25—28° C
Sponge consistency:	Same as main dough

Sponge ripeness:	the sponge should have risen well and be on the verge of collapse

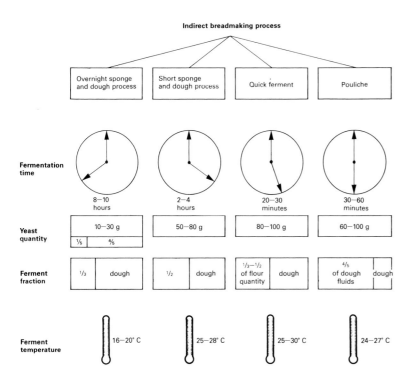

The quick ferment

Especialy suitable for very rich doughs. The gluten in the ferment is able to swell and there-by produces an elastic, pliable main dough.

Fermentation time:	20—30 minutes
Ferment fraction:	$1/3$—$1/2$ of the main dough
Yeast quantity:	80—100 g per liter of fluids
Ferment temperature:	25—30° C
Water temperature for fermentation:	35—40° C
Ferment consistency:	approximately 2 kg flour per liter of fluids
Ferment ripeness:	the ripe ferment will rise to the surface of the water and float.

The ferment is moulded into the shape of a ring and is placed in warm water. After 10—15 minutes the ring is turned. After another 10—15 minutes the dough is ripe enough to be used in the main dough. It must be indicated that the ferment will absorb water and this must be taken into account when weighing up the ingredients for the main dough.

The pouliche

Suitable for products with a smooth crumb and a crisp crust.

Fermentation time:	$1/2$—1 hour
Ferment fraction:	$4/5$ of the total fluid quantity
Yeast quantity:	60—100 g per liter of fluids
Ferment temperature:	24—27° C
Ferment consistency:	500 g flour per liter of fluids
Ferment ripeness:	the ferment is considered ripe when an intensive formation of bubbles seen on the surface.

The pouliche is mixed together with a whisk and is left to stand at room temperature.

The direct breadmaking process

In contrast to the indirect breadmaking process all the ingredients are *directly* mixed to a dough. There are three direct breadmaking processes, each of which is suitable for the production of certain products. One can distinguish between:
— the long direct fermentation process
— the short direct fermentation process
— the quick or express method

The long direct fermentation process

This method is mainly used for large breads and laminated doughs, it is seldom used for small breads. This method is similar to the overnight sponge and dough process. The lengthy fermentation time can have its disadvantages, depending on the flour quality, the fermentation time and the dough temperature. In order to overcome these it is recommended to keep the dough as cool as possible.

Fermentation time:	8—10 hours
Yeast quantity:	15—25 g per liter of fluids for large breads 40—60 g per liter of fluids for small breads and special breads
Dough temperature:	14—18° C
Dough consistency:	according to the type of bread being made

The short direct fermentation process

This is the most common method of dough fermentation and is suitable for the production of most breads, special breads and small breads. This method requires a minimal amount of work, saves time, does not require much dough supervision, reduces the weight loss due to fermentation and produces a uniform bread quality. This method also has its disadvantages — minimal development of aroma and flavour as well as rapid staling of the baked product.

Fermentation time: 1—3 hours
Yeast quantity: 40—60 g per liter of fluids for large breads
       60—80 g per liter of fluids for small breads and special breads
Dough temperature: 22—24° C
Proving cabinet
temperature: 24—27° C
Dough consistency: according to the product being made

Because these doughs have a short fermentation time they have to be mixed intensively. The dough is knocked back in order to achieve the required stability and fermentation power. To improve the product quality it is possible to add bread improvers (e. g. Levit).

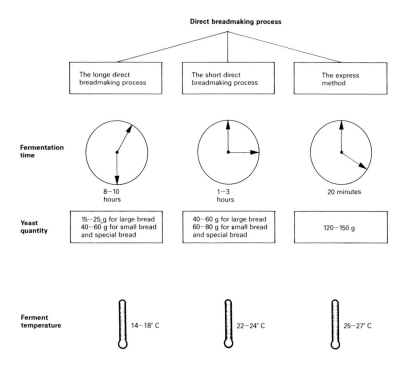

The express method

The development and construction of new mixing machines has enabled the introduction of new mixing methods. The conventional methods require a biological ripening of the dough where-as the modern intensive mixing processes cause a mechanical ripening. This enables the doughs to be moulded directly after mixing. This method is suitable for the production of small breads and is carried out as follows:

Fermentation time: 10—20 minutes
Yeast quantity: 120—150 g per liter of fluids
Dough temperature: 25—27° C
Dough consistency: normal

The product quality can be improved if the correct bread improvers are added.

If the salt is added after half of the mixing time the dough will become plastic and an improvement will be seen in the fermentation power, the dough development and the structure of the baked product. The dough should be moulded directly after mixing.

It is important that the dough temperature be kept between 25—27° C, so that a normal, final proof can take place. With the express method, it requires only 30 minutes final proof before the products are ready for baking.

Dough retarding

This process is based on temporarily lowering the temperature of the moulded dough to freezing point (+2° C to —2° C). It requires an adjustable cooling cell with a relative humidity of 70—85%. The retarding process can be controlled as desired. After retarding the temperature is slowly raised and the dough is allowed to thaw out. The dough is then warmed so that a normal final proof can take place. If this process is properly regulated and controlled the baker can bake according to his needs.

Dough production

Mixing time: Depending on the type of machine, 12—16 minutes. It is important that a careful but complete dough mixing process is carried out.
Dough consistency: Slightly tighter than a normal dough. This means a yield reduction of 2—3%.
Yeast quantity: 20—25 g per liter for large breads
       40—70 g per liter for small breads and special breads
Fermentation time: moulding immediately after mixing
Baking temperature: 15—20° C less than normal
Bread improvers: In order to prevent wide flowing doughs, bread improvers containing asorbic acid should be added.

Dough Preparation

Dough processing

In order to produce a product of outstanding quality the following points must be taken into account:
- The exact weighing up of all the ingredients
- The correct processing of all the ingredients − in the right order
- Ingredients such as fats, sesame seeds, poppy seeds, linseeds etc. should be added towards the end of the mixing process.
- Nuts, kernels and fruits should be carefully added after the dough mixing. The fruits should be washed and soaked beforehand. On adding to the dough they should be dried of excess water so that they can easily be incorporated into the dough.

The mixing process

Optimal dough development during mixing requires the following factors:
- Flour quality
  Intensive mixing of strong flours, careful mixing of weak flours.
- Dough consistency
  Tight doughs develop quicker than soft doughs.
- Dough temperature
  High temperatures cause the protein to swell quickly.
- Dough ingredients
  An enriched dough takes longer to develop.
- Dough fermentation
  A short fermentation time requires a longer mixing process because the dough must then be developed mechanically.
- Mixing machine
  The optimal mixing times are:
  a) at 28−40 rotations per minute, 25−30 minutes
  b) at 80−120 rotations per minute, 8−12 minutes
  c) at 1400−2800 rotations per minute, 1−2 minutes

These different machines cause the dough temperature to rise at different rates. The mechanical dough warming can be corrected by lowering the temperature of the water to be added.
By taking a piece of dough with both hands and stretching it to a thin film one can test the dough's development. The thinner the film the more developed it is.

Dough temperature

The ideal temperature of a yeast dough is 24−26° C. In order to prevent a dough from skinning or forming a crust, one must keep it's temperature 1−2° C below room temperature. A dough shows good fermentation power when it's temperature rises by 1−2° C during fermentation. The yeast quantity should be measused according to the dough temperature. It is advantageous to control a dough with a long fermentation period by reducing the dough temperature rather than by reducing the addition of yeast.

Final proving

This process has a great influence on the final appearance and taste of a product. However the final proof also depends on the dough ingredients, the type of product and the baking temperature. The following points must be regarded closely:
- Tight doughs require a longer final proof.
- Doughs to be cut should be placed in the oven after a short fermentation time.
- Products requiring a smooth surface need a long final proof.
- The final proof also depends on the oven temperature. For a cold oven a short final proof is required and for a hot oven a long final proof

Baking

Correct baking is of vital importance. The most important factors are:
- The correct oven temperature for each type of bread
- The ability to recognise the optimal final proof of a dough
- The correct cutting for various types of bread
- The correct amount of steaming and the correct timing and pulling of the steam dampers
- Careful baking of the bread

Cantonal and regional breads

Almost every Canton, sometimes even half-canton, knows specific types of bread which have been handed down the years. In the last century these types have gained in popularity and so the production of many types has spread out over the various Canton borders, and so have become known throughout whole Regions. Others however are today seldom seen even in the Canton whose name they bear.

General method of production

Flour

Dark flour and half-white flour are mainly used for Cantonal breads however white flour, rye flour and coarse whole rye meal are sometimes also used.

Dough production and dough temperature

Flour which is short of gluten or which has a weak gluten will take less kneading and need greater care in mixing. With the indirect method care must be taken that the sponge is worked well first. Flour rich in gluten or with strong gluten needs a more intensive kneading.
The kneading time, as with the water temperature has to be regulated according to the type of machine being used. In this way the best temperature needed for the dough development and the fermentation can be achieved.

Fermentation method

For the production of large bread types the indirect method with sponge or the direct straight dough is used.

Dough handling

With weaker flours the knocking back of the fermenting dough, once or twice, is an advantage, but with stronger flours knocking back is only advised with very soft doughs. This will make them stronger and drier.

Fermentation process

Basically, a long bulk fermentation is necessary for the build-up of flavour, while the individual final proof is of less importance. This can be between 20 to 30 minutes according to flour type, bread sort and dough consistency. Bakery additives such as Levit; which is a product developed by the Richemont Craft School; will give added flavour. Apart from this a correct dosage will give an effective protection against the various bread diseases.

Working off

When moulding the dough it is important to see to it that each piece is evenly stretched. The moulded bread pieces are then to be placed either directly onto the oven sets, or onto cloths according to the type of loaf. The working of each bread sort is explained next to the appropriate picture.

Baking

Baking off plays an important role. The most important points to note when baking are:
— the correct oven temperature for each bread type
— an understanding of the optimum proof time for each piece
— a correct cut on top of each article
— the correct quantity of steam and the early removal of that steam
— a careful baking off.

Recipe

For the Canton bread of Aargau, Appenzell, Bern, Genf, Glarus, Jura, Luzern, Neuenburg, Nidwalden, Obwalden, St. Gallen, Schaffhausen, Schwyz, Thurgau, Zug, Uri, Waadt and Zürich.

Short straight dough fermentation (for medium stiff dough)

	Dark bread	Half-white bread
Water	10,000 kg	10,000 kg
Yeast	0,400 kg	0,400 kg
Levit	0,200 kg	0,200 kg
Salt	0,350 kg	0,400 kg
Flour	approx. 14,000 kg	approx. 15,000 kg

Knead the dough thoroughly. Dough temperature 22 to 25°C. Bulk ferment 60 to 75 minutes.

Long straight dough fermentation (recipe for medium stiff dough)

	Dark bread	Half-white bread
Water	10,000 kg	10,000 kg
Yeast	0,150 kg	0,150 kg
Levit	0,100 kg	0,100 kg
Salt	0,350 kg	0,400 kg
Flour	approx. 15,000 kg	approx. 16,000 kg

Knead the dough sufficiently, but carefully. Dough temperature 16 to 20°C. Bulk fermentation 6 to 8 hours.

Indirect fermentation (recipe for medium stiff dough)

Ferment	Dark bread	Half-white bread
Water	3,000 kg	3,000 kg
Yeast	0,075 kg	0,075 kg
Flour	approx. 4,200 kg	approx. 4,500 kg

Dough	Dark bread	Half-white bread
Water	7,000 kg	7,000 kg
Yeast	0,320 kg	0,320 kg
Salt	0,350 kg	0,400 kg
Flour	approx. 10,000 kg	approx. 11,000 kg

Knead the ferment well. Dough temperature 16 to 20°C. Ferment 6 to 8 hours.
Eventually knead well together with the remaining ingredients. Dough temperature 22 to 25°C. Bulk fermentation up to 60 minutes.

Recipe

For the Canton bread of Basel-city, Basel-country, Solothurn. They are different to the other recipes because of the higher water content.

Water content

Bread type	Dark bread	Half-white bread
Basel bread	76 to 85%	75 to 82%
Solothurn bread	74 to 82%	72 to 80%

Dough Handling

It is of the greatest importance when handling these soft to very soft doughs to knock them back several times during the fermentation period in order to improve their stability as much as possible.

Aargau bread

Originally native to the Canton Aargau it is seldom produced today.

Dough

Medium stiff dark or half-white bread dough.

Working off

After the first round moulding, shape the pieces to a long oval form. Enclose in cloths with the closure uppermost. After a moderate proof turn them over, cut deeply to a slight «S» shape and put into a not too hot oven. After baking brush immediately with hot water or a starch glaze.

Basel bread

This differs from the other Canton bread types in many ways. Firstly because of the soft dough which is produced and the coarse uneven crumb texture which results and secondly from its special, typical taste which is created by the aromas which build up in the floury, crispy crust.

Dough

```
10,000 kg water
 0,500 kg yeast
 0,200 kg Levit
 0,400 kg salt
11,500 kg half-white or dark
         flour, approx.
```

Method

Work the ingredients to a dough. Dough temperature 20 to 22°C. Bulk fermentation 60 to 90 minutes and during this time knock the dough back lightly twice. In this way the dough will become more stable.

Working off

Work off the weighed pieces to long oval shapes and place with the closure uppermost onto heavily dusted dough boards.
After a good proof turn the pieces over and place in pairs, with the joining ends pushed lightly together, on the canvas setters. Place in a very hot oven with steam and then bake out strongly with the open damper.

Bern bread

The production of Bern bread is not limited to the one area, it is made in other Cantons under the general name of «Round bread».

Dough

Medium stiff dark or half-white bread dough.

Method

Mould the dough into a short, oval form. Leave to recover for five minutes and roll up tightly. Cover with a cloth and leave to prove with the closure facing downwards. After a short proving time cut deeply across the width and place in a steamed oven. Bake-off with an open steam-damper. The bread should have a splendid rip and the base should have the shape of the figure eight (8). After baking glaze with hot water.

43

Bündner rye bread

The rye bread ring is a bakery shape of ancient origin which is still made today in mountain farms and then kept on a stick for weeks, or even months as a stored food.

In the south in Puschlav the ring bread is called Brasciadela. There it is made mostly from half-white rye flour and flavoured also with aniseed.

For rye rings at least two thirds of the flour quantity must consist of rye flour. The remaining third can consist of wheat flour in order to give the dough better baking properties.

Recipe

Straight dough

3,000 kg water
0,150 kg yeast
0,150 kg Levit
0,100 kg salt
3,600 kg rye flour, half-white
0,900 kg dark flour

Indirect dough method

Sponge dough

1,000 kg water
0,050 kg ferment
1,500 kg rye flour, half-white

Dough

2,500 kg sponge dough
2,000 kg water
0,150 kg yeast
0,100 kg salt
2,000 kg rye flour, half-white
1,000 kg dark flour

Method

Ferment the sponge for 6 to 8 hours.
Kneading time 5 to 6 minutes.
Bulk fermentation time 40 to 50 minutes.

Working off

Weigh off dough pieces of 600 g, lightly hand up round and then gently mould out long to about 40 to 45 cm. Fasten the two ends together. Place on rye flour dusted boards with the closure uppermost. Prove for about 20 minutes. Before setting in the oven cut three times with a blade and then put in the oven with steam. After a few minutes remove the steam. Baking time 40 to 45 minutes.

Freiburg bread

A type of bread which today is made from wheat and rye flour but which had its origins in the Sense area and is known as «Rüa-bread».

Dough

A medium tight dough made from a mixture of ⅓ each of dark, half-white and half-white rye flours.

Production

Mould the dough pieces round and place on cloths. When half proved flatten slightly and mark into squares with a stick. Finish proving and then bake in a moderate oven.

Genf bread

Genf bread has an extremely flat shape. When well baked out it gets a similar crust structure to that of the Paris bread, thanks to its minimal crumb structure.

Dough

A medium tight dough of half-white flour.

Production

Mould the dough pieces round, dust well with flour, press out flat and after a short rest pin out evenly with the rolling pin. After a good proof cut the whole top surface to diamond shapes. Bake out fully in a medium oven.

Glarus bread

This type of bread has not found favour outside its own Canton. The people of Glarus however place value on this long-oval bread with its large split, above all because of its large crust area.

Dough

Medium dark or half-white bread dough.

Production

Work off the dough pieces to long rolls and place on cloths with the closure uppermost. Cut deeply before placing in the oven.
Bake in a medium oven and brush immediately with hot water.

Jura bread

When the Canton of Jura was founded the Master Bakers created this new, decorative Canton bread. In its shape the Jura bread has a certain similarity to those from Genf, the Waadtland Carrelé and the Wallis rye bread. The Jura bread with its curved shape appeals above all with its fine and crisp crust.

Dough

Medium tight dark or half-white bread dough.

Production

Place the round moulded pieces onto cloths and after a short rest press out lightly to flat shapes. After half proof notch in the contours of the Jura coat-of-arms and dust with a little flour. Bake in a medium hot oven.

49

Luzern bread

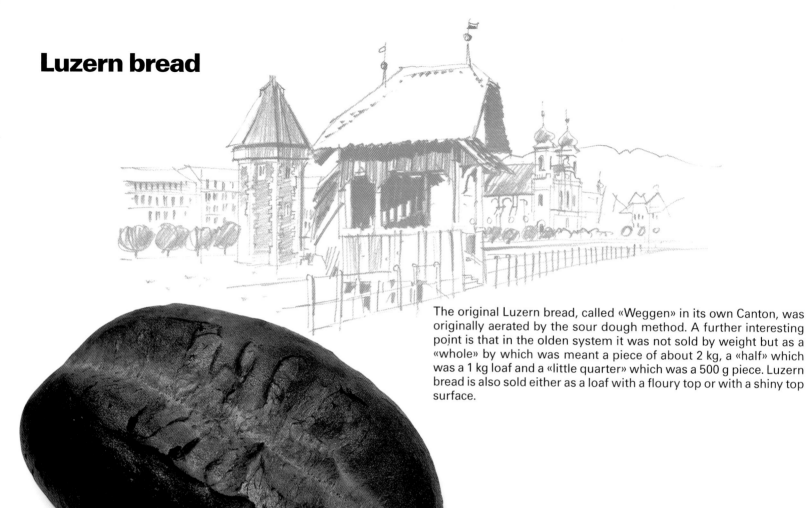

The original Luzern bread, called «Weggen» in its own Canton, was originally aerated by the sour dough method. A further interesting point is that in the olden system it was not sold by weight but as a «whole» by which was meant a piece of about 2 kg, a «half» which was a 1 kg loaf and a «little quarter» which was a 500 g piece. Luzern bread is also sold either as a loaf with a floury top or with a shiny top surface.

Recipe with sour dough

Sponge dough

3,000 kg water
0,500 kg ferment
4,500 kg dark flour

Fermentation: approx.
6–8 hours at 26 to 28°C.

Dough

8,000 kg sponge dough
7,000 kg water
0,300 kg salt
10,000 kg dark flour

Method

Mix the ingredients to a dough. Dough temperature 26 to 28°C. Bulk fermentation time 60 to 90 minutes.

Working off

Mould the dough pieces to oval long shapes and place on cloths. After half proof press down once along the length. Bake in a fairly hot oven to a good dark brown.

Neuenburg bread

Baked off as a double piece, the Neuenburg bread is split and sold as single pieces with one end having no crust.

Dough

A rather softer half-white bread dough.

Production

First hand up loosely and after a short rest mould out tightly. Place two together with the closure underneath onto cloths and cover over to prove. After a good proof bake the bread in a medium oven. Glaze with hot water.

Nidwalden bread

Although the two half-Cantons Ob- and Nidwalden are next to each other the bread shapes are basically quite different.

Dough

Medium tight dough of dark or half-white flour.

Production

Hand up the dough pieces, round lightly, then finish moulding tightly and place onto cloths. After a medium proof cut deeply with the blade held at an angle. This gives the bread the typical broad oval shape. Put in a moderately hot oven and after baking brush with hot water.

Obwalden bread

The bread has the folk name of «Stecken bread» because of its long stretched-out baton shape. The smooth crust and the two open ends are typical for the Obwalden bread.

Dough

A rather softer dark or half-white bread dough.

Production

Pre-mould the dough piece to a long shape and then evenly, tightly lengthen out to approx. 50 cm and place in pairs to join at the ends. Allow to stand covered and after a very good proof bake in a medium warm oven. Glaze with hot water.

Schaffhausen bread

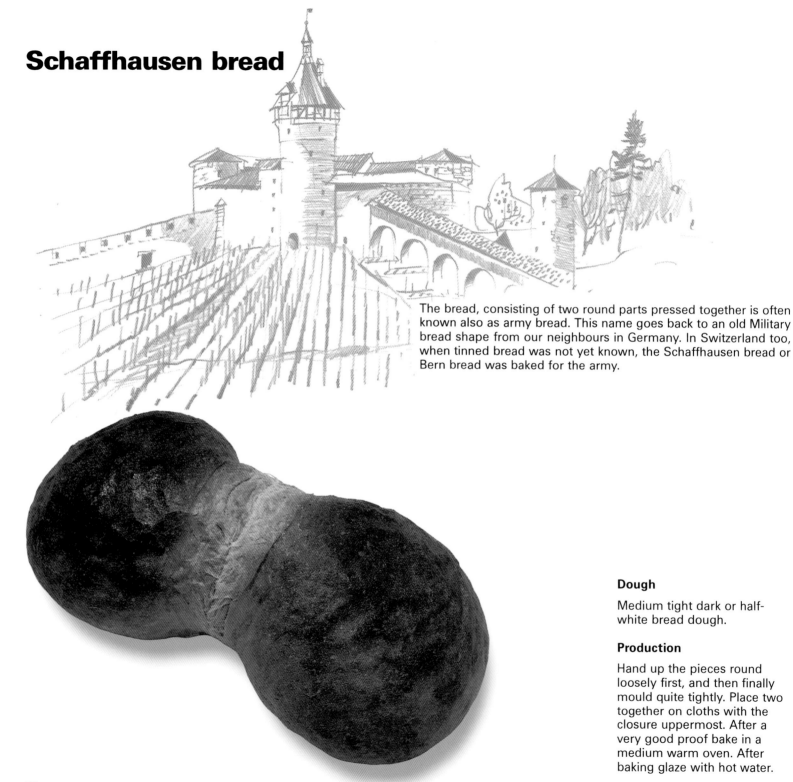

The bread, consisting of two round parts pressed together is often known also as army bread. This name goes back to an old Military bread shape from our neighbours in Germany. In Switzerland too, when tinned bread was not yet known, the Schaffhausen bread or Bern bread was baked for the army.

Dough

Medium tight dark or half-white bread dough.

Production

Hand up the pieces round loosely first, and then finally mould quite tightly. Place two together on cloths with the closure uppermost. After a very good proof bake in a medium warm oven. After baking glaze with hot water.

54

Solothurn bread

Very similar to Basel bread, Solothurn bread can be produced from the same dough. It is however made as single pieces, which should be allowed to burst out on the sides during the baking process. This creation at the side, highly prized by some customers, is achieved by the way in which the dough is put into the oven.

Dough

Soft dark or half-white bread dough.

Production

Carefully fold the dough together and place on heavily floured boards. After little proof turn over carefully and bake in a hot oven without cutting.

St. Gallen, Appenzell and Thurgau bread

The St. Gallen bread has a shape which is entirely unique and is not to be found anywhere else; which requires a lot of skill and routine from the baker.

The St. Gallen bread should burst open freely on the front and have a «nose» over the break. It should be glazed immediately after baking. Those who like a tight crumb and delightful crust will be highly satisfied with the St. Gallen bread.

Appenzell and Thurgau bread is identical to the St. Gallen bread in practice, right from the dough production to the baking. Both Cantons are mostly country in type with large families living there, so that the bread is baked often in large heavy pieces of up to five pounds in weight, which also then require special high baking ovens.

Dough

Medium tight dark or half-white bread dough.

Working off

Hand up the dough pieces lightly and place on wooden boards. After a moderate proof work off to the typical St. Galler shape as shown in the sketch. Place two or more of the loaves on the setting apparatus and cut with the knife directly under the middle piece horizontally to create the «nose». Any blisters which might occur during the moulding and shaping should be removed with the docker. After baking glaze immediately with hot water.

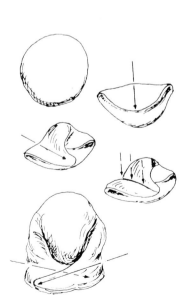

Schwyz and Zug bread

(Head bread)

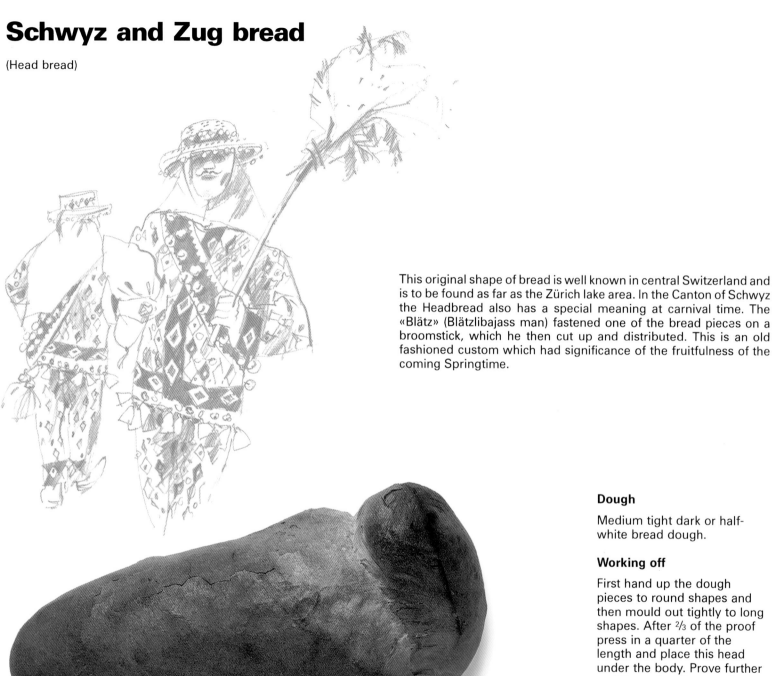

This original shape of bread is well known in central Switzerland and is to be found as far as the Zürich lake area. In the Canton of Schwyz the Headbread also has a special meaning at carnival time. The «Blätz» (Blätzlibajass man) fastened one of the bread pieces on a broomstick, which he then cut up and distributed. This is an old fashioned custom which had significance of the fruitfulness of the coming Springtime.

Dough

Medium tight dark or half-white bread dough.

Working off

First hand up the dough pieces to round shapes and then mould out tightly to long shapes. After ⅔ of the proof press in a quarter of the length and place this head under the body. Prove further and then place in a moderate oven with the closure underneath and the head uppermost. After baking glaze with hot water.

58

Uri bread

In the Canton Uri this bread is called «Halberli» (Little half), because it is put together from two equal pieces. During the baking process the Uri bread achieves a fine break at the point of contact of the two pieces and this gives a good crust, with the strong baking off process.

Dough

Medium tight dark or half-white bread dough.

Production

Mould the dough pieces round and place on cloths. After a good proof place in pairs, lightly touching each other, in a moderate oven and bake off.

Tessin bread

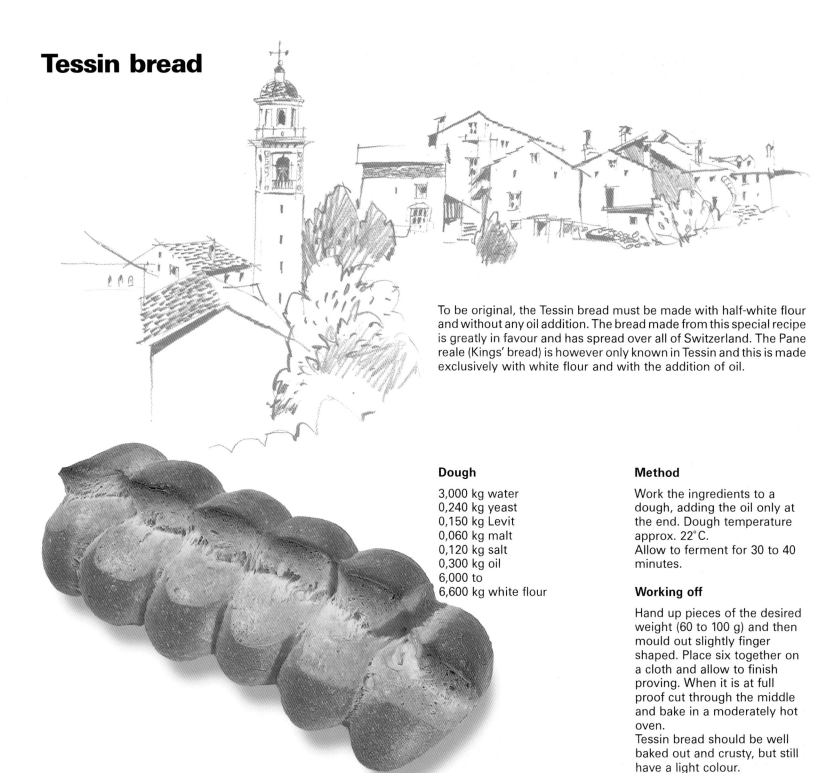

To be original, the Tessin bread must be made with half-white flour and without any oil addition. The bread made from this special recipe is greatly in favour and has spread over all of Switzerland. The Pane reale (Kings' bread) is however only known in Tessin and this is made exclusively with white flour and with the addition of oil.

Dough

3,000 kg water
0,240 kg yeast
0,150 kg Levit
0,060 kg malt
0,120 kg salt
0,300 kg oil
6,000 to
6,600 kg white flour

Method

Work the ingredients to a dough, adding the oil only at the end. Dough temperature approx. 22°C.
Allow to ferment for 30 to 40 minutes.

Working off

Hand up pieces of the desired weight (60 to 100 g) and then mould out slightly finger shaped. Place six together on a cloth and allow to finish proving. When it is at full proof cut through the middle and bake in a moderately hot oven.
Tessin bread should be well baked out and crusty, but still have a light colour.

Waadt cross bread

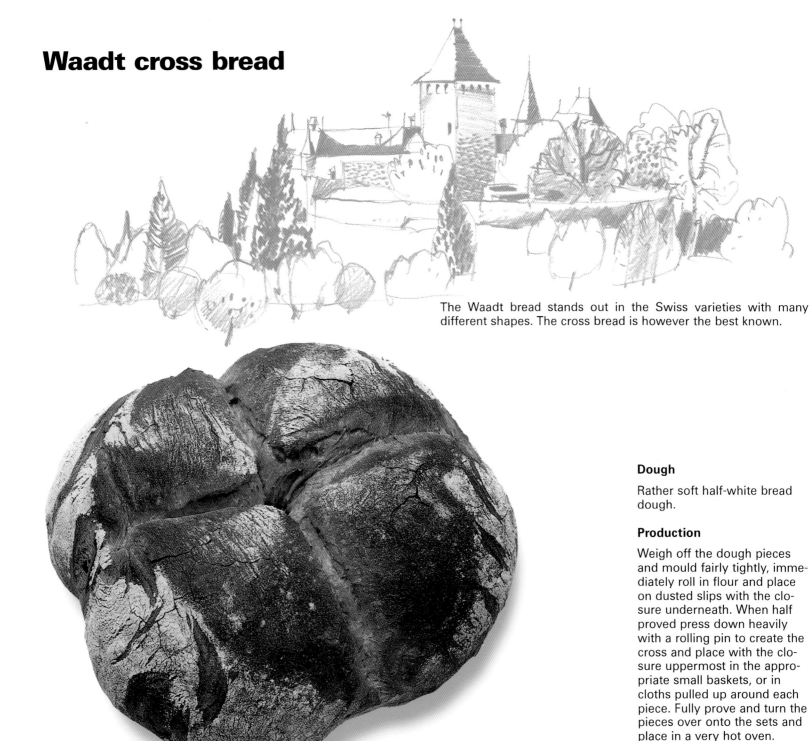

The Waadt bread stands out in the Swiss varieties with many different shapes. The cross bread is however the best known.

Dough

Rather soft half-white bread dough.

Production

Weigh off the dough pieces and mould fairly tightly, immediately roll in flour and place on dusted slips with the closure underneath. When half proved press down heavily with a rolling pin to create the cross and place with the closure uppermost in the appropriate small baskets, or in cloths pulled up around each piece. Fully prove and turn the pieces over onto the sets and place in a very hot oven. When the loaf is set, open the damper and finish baking out.

Wallis rye bread

This rustical bread with its own very strong flavour is well liked, cut in thin slices, to eat with cheese, dried meat and sausages.
The original Wallis bread was made from sour dough starter.
It keeps fresh for a long period, although when made with yeast its keeping properties are reduced slightly.

Recipe with sour dough

Sponge dough

1,000 kg water
0,050 kg sour dough starter
1,500 kg fine rye grain flour

Dough

2,200 kg Sponge dough
2,000 kg water
0,100 kg salt
2,800 kg fine rye grain flour

Method

Knead the ferment with the other ingredients to a dough. Bulk fermentation 40 to 60 minutes.

Working off

Weigh off the dough as desired and hand up round. Roll the pieces completely on all sides into rye flour, and place on dusted boards with the closure underneath. Press out a little flat and allow to prove. The correct proof is shown by the even breaks which occur all over the top surface. Bake the bread out well in a not-too-hot oven.

Zürich bread

Zürich bread, commonly called Long bread is one of the most widely known bread types in Switzerland, because of its practical shape which allows it to be easily cut into even sized pieces. It is very convenient for restaurants and cafes where it is often supplied in a longer shape with its own trade name or as stick bread.

Dough

Medium tight dark or half-white bread dough.

Working off

First hand the pieces up round and then tightly into long loaves. Place on cloths with the closure uppermost or directly onto setting boards. After a good proof cut the top surface 3 to 5 times with the blade held flat at an angle. After baking out, glaze immediately with water.

Special breads

Special breads

Special working requirements

The production of bread using dark or half-white flours with a few other ingredients is completely in contrast to that of special breads which can use a great number of different flours and other raw materials.

The craft baker has to take into account the effect of the factors brought into play by these ingredients on the dough preparation, the fermentation, the working off and the baking properties.

Although the special breads have differing recipes within the groups in the production framework, there are certain basic rules concerning the main raw material being used.

Whole wheat bread

The meal flour which is mostly supplied with medium to coarse granulation needs plenty of time in the mixing and preparation for it to take up the water i.e. to soak the individual grain particles and to develop the gluten.

So, whole wheat doughs need a very good, long process of careful dough mixing with a very slow speed. Although mostly baked in tins it still demands an optimium mixing and a following long cool fermentation period to improve the consistency of the dough which will then play a big part in the elasticity and cutting properties of the crumb. The bulk fermentation period however must not be stretched out too much, otherwise there will be an enzymic breakdown of the dough particles. Even, firm moulding is required for the tin bread. Whole wheat bread is baked after full proof in a well steamed oven of medium temperature. After at least half of the baking time it is an advantage to remove the bread from the tins and finish baking it with an open damper to allow a crust to be formed on the sides of the loaves.

Bread from white and half-white flours

Doughs made from light flours need an intensive working because of their higher quality of gluten and the greater strength of that gluten. A cool, rather shorter period of fermentation is recommended for most sorts of this group. With Paris bread however the bulk fermentation should be considerably increased with an appropriate reduction in the yeast quantity, in order to achieve the necessary short crumb structure. The characteristics of the bread have to be taken into account during its working. While Paris bread and Bürli bread only need to be worked off loosely and without forcing it, for toast and cut bread a typical tight and firm dough is needed.

The differences are also to be noted in the baking. The most liked bread in the West and South of Switzerland are the ones with a higher proportion of light but crisp crust. In contrast to this the Bürli bread is given a dark, strong and crisp crust by being baked in a very hot oven.

Bread from different flours and additives

The recipes in this group are mostly made up with darker flours and the method of work can seldom be identified.

They show the greatest variety in their make-up and are geared to the physiological aspect of nutrition. So it is necessary to follow the recipes and methods correctly to obtain the specific results for each type, through from mixing to baking.

Rye bread

Care must be taken in the work because of consideration of the various methods of working properties of the rye flour, especially with regard to the mixing process. Rye doughs become too runny if worked too much and so they must be worked with great care until the dough just leaves the sides of the mixing bowl. It is important that rye bread doughs are sufficiently ripe and therefore only an indirect breadmaking process should be used.

The dough temperature needs to be kept some 4 to 6°C higher than is the case with most of the special breads which have been shown up to this point.

The ferment, which must be kept cold for technical reasons, will otherwise have too great an influence on the fermentation process. The bulk fermentation time should not exceed 60 minutes as the mild acid produced at that time does not help with producing a good dough stability. The basically low tolerance to fermentation of rye dough needs an optimal match to the final proof of the individual loaves. Rye bread as a general rule should be baked in a moderate to hot oven with steam at the start. When the loaf has expanded and set the steam should be removed and the bread then well baked out.

Bread from whole wheat flour

Five corn bread

(fine and coarse)

Dough

3000 g water
250 g yeast
120 g Levit
90 g salt
3800 g five corn flour fine
or
3900 g five corn flour, coarse

Dough temperature 22 to 24°C.

Method

Knead the ingredients to a dough.
Bulk fermentation max. 45 minutes.

Working off

Work off the dough pieces, round and then to long shapes. Allow to prove in greased tins for 25 to 30 minutes. Spray the fully proved loaves with water before putting them into the oven. Bake for approx. 40 minutes in a not-too-hot oven, remove from the tins and bake out for a further 15 to 20 minutes.

Whole wheat bread

Sponge dough

1 500 g water
10 g yeast
2 000 g whole wheat flour

Knead thoroughly.
Ferment temperature 18 to
20°C.
Fermentation time 4 hours.

Dough

1 500 g water
150 g yeast
90 g salt
2 000 g whole wheat flour

Dough temperature 26 to
28°C.

Method

Mix the ingredients with the
sponge ferment into a dough
and knead well. The dough
should have a compact and
long structure.
Fermentation time 60 minutes.

Working off

Weigh off pieces appropriate
to the size of basket and
mould to long shapes.

When the pieces reach full
proof put in a good hot oven
with steam. Let the steam out
after a few minutes in order to
avoid the loaves breaking
open at the sides.

Graham bread

Straight dough

Dough

3 000 g water
60 g yeast
150 g Levit
15 g malt
90 g salt
3 900 g whole wheat meal, fine
coarsed

Dough temperature 22 to
24°C.

Indirect Fermentation

Sponge dough

1 600 g water
20 g yeast
2 000 g whole wheat meal, fine
coarsed

Knead well together.
Sponge temperature approx.
18°C.
Fermentation time 6 to
8 hours.

Dough

7 000 g sponge dough
400 g water
50 g yeast
60 g salt
500 g whole wheat meal, fine
coarsed

Dough temperature 22 to
24°C.

Method

Knead the ingredients well to
a dough.
Bulk fermentation 60 minutes.

Working off

Hand up the weighed pieces
round and then shape out
long and place in greased tins.
When fully proved place in a
medium hot, presteamed
oven. When half baked
remove the bread from the
tins and finish baking with an
open damper.

Bread from white and half-white flour

Paris bread

Dough

3000 g water
75 g yeast
60 g Levit
60 g malt
100 g salt
4800 g white flour

Dough temperature approx. 24°C.

Method

Break down the yeast, Levit and malt in the water and knead to a dough with the flour. Add the salt towards the end and finish kneading the dough.
Bulk fermentation 2 to 2½ hours.

Working off

Weigh off dough pieces at 600 g and mould out half long. After a short recovery period carefully roll out to strands of 70 cm. Do not force them out too quickly. Place the pieces onto the sets with the closure to the bottom and leave to

Parisette, Ficelles

prove. When fully proved cut
five or six times with a blade
held flat to the surface.
Place in a medium hot oven
with steam and then bake off
with an open damper.

Dough

3000 g water
  200 g yeast
  100 g Levit
   60 g malt
  100 g salt
4800 g white flour

Dough temperature 22 to
24°C.

Method

Break down the yeast, Levit
and malt in the water and
knead to a dough with the
flour. Add the salt at the end
of the process and finish
kneading the dough.
Bulk fermentation 45 to
60 minutes.

PARISETTE

Working off

Weigh off pieces of 320 g and
mould up tightly and fashion
to 30 cm long. Place on cloths
with the closure uppermost
and leave to prove fully.
Before baking, turn the Pari-
settes over and cut three
times with the blade held flat
and the cuts being diagonal.
Put in a medium hot oven with
plenty of steam and then
finish baking with an open
damper.

FICELLES

Working off

Weigh off dough pieces of
400 g and hand up round.
Then fashion to thin dough
sticks of 90 cm long. Place
directly onto the oven setters
and prove well. Before putting
in the oven cut short notches
with a sharp knife. Bake in a
medium hot oven with pre-
steaming and finish off crisply
with an open damper.

Cornetti, Mailand bread, Ciampa Locarnese

Dough

3 000 g water
  250 g yeast
  100 g Levit
   60 g malt
  150 g salt
6 000 g white flour, approx.
  300 g oil

Dough temperature 22 to 24°C.

Method

Break down the yeast, Levit and malt in the water and knead with the flour. When half made up add the oil. Add the salt almost at the end of the kneading time, and then knead well.
Fermentation time approx. 20 minutes.

CORNETTI

Working off

Using the machine, roll out the individual pieces into bands of 2,5 mm and lightly dust with rye flour. Roll up tightly from both ends and place two pieces together to a Cornetti shape.

Place directly onto sheets, cover with plastic and allow to prove. Place in a medium hot oven with steam and finish off baking to a light colour with an open damper. Do not brush the Cornetti. They should have a light floury, crisp but light coloured crust.

MAILAND BREAD

Working off

Weigh off as for Cornetti dough and work off long shapes. After a short recovery, roll out to long bands, then roll up tightly from the one side. The spirals must be kept visible. Allow the pieces to prove well and before baking cut deeply across the top surface. Put in a medium hot oven with steam and then bake off crisply with an open damper, but bake off to a light colour.

CIAMPA LOCARNESE

Working off

Work off long pieces of Cornetti dough and leave to recover a little. With the rolling pin or machine roll out down the length to strips 2 to 3 mm thick and lightly dust with rye flour.
Roll up both ends to the middle evenly until they touch each other. Press across the centre with a rolling pin. Pull two sides lightly apart and place the two opposite lying parts between. Place on cloths or directly onto the oven sets. When fully proved turn them over, put in the oven with steam and then bake off to a crisp but light coloured crust, with an open damper.

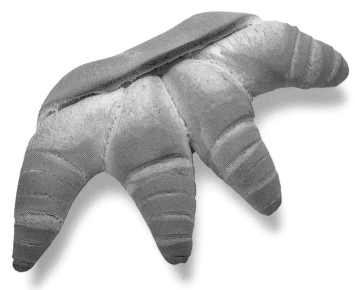

Bürli bread

Schilt bread

Sponge dough

1 000 g water
10 g yeast
45 g Levit
1 300 g half-white flour

Dough

2 500 g sponge dough
2 000 g water
60 g yeast
100 g salt
2 000 g half-white flour

Dough temperature 22 to 24°C.

Method

Allow the sponge to stand for 2 to 3 hours and then knead with the rest of the ingredients. Knock back two or three times during the bulk fermentation of 1 to 2 hours. The dough must be very soft but stable.

Working off

Break off dough pieces and place on dusted boards. After a good proof lightly place them over the length; place them in a hot oven with steam and bake off with an open damper.

Dough

3 000 g water
180 g yeast
100 g Levit
60 g malt
100 g salt
5 400 g white flour

Dough temperature 22 to 24°C.

Method

Make a medium stiff dough from these ingredients. Bulk fermentation 1½ to 2 hours.

Working off

Weigh off dough pieces at 100 to 120 g, hand up round and then allow to rest a little. Eventually work to a slightly conical shape. Dip the thick part in rye flour and place in fours to form the Schilt. Place on cloths with the closure uppermost and allow to prove fully. Turn over before putting them in a good hot oven with steam, lifting them up slightly in the centre as this is done. Finish baking with the damper open. After baking brush with hot water.

Toast bread, Model bread

Dough

3000 g milk
  250 g yeast
  150 g Levit
   60 g malt
  120 g salt
6000 g white flour
  450 g butter

Dough temperature 22 to 24°C.

Method

Knead the ingredients to a dough. Add the butter ¾ of the way through the process and the salt at the end. Work off as soon as the kneading process is complete.

TOAST BREAD

Working off

Hand up the weighed off pieces and then mould to the length of the tins to be used, and place in the greased tins. Close the tins and allow to prove. After full proof bake in a moderate oven.
After baking tip out immediately onto wires.

MODEL BREAD

Working off

Work up the dough pieces, place into greased cake tins and leave to prove. After three quarter proof brush with egg and when fully proved bake in a medium hot oven.

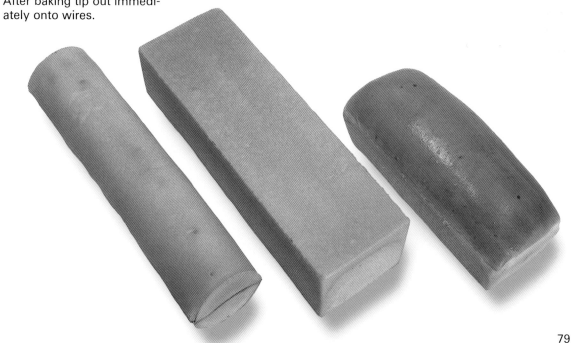

Farmer bread

Bread from various flours and additives

Dough

1 500 g water
1 500 g milk
  250 g yeast
  150 g Levit
  100 g salt
2 800 g dark flour
1 100 g rye flour
     or
3 900 g Farmer flour
    ($2/3$ dark flour, $1/3$ dark rye flours)
Dough temperature 22 to 24°C.

Method

Using the ingredients make to a dough with not-too-stiff a consistency.
Bulk fermentation 70 to 90 minutes.

Working off

Weigh off the dough pieces and hand up tightly round. Place these with the closure uppermost onto flour dusted boards and turn over after a full proof. Cut the floury top surface crossways. Place in a good hot oven. When set, replace in a medium hot oven to bake out. The Farmer bread must have a strong crispy crust.

Rustico bread

Dough

3 000 g cold water
1 100 g coarse whole wheat
          meal
1 100 g coarse whole rye meal,
          fine to medium

Mix together and allow to
stand for 10 to 12 hours.

  200 g yeast
  150 g Levit
  120 g salt
2 300 g half-white flour

Dough temperature 22 to
24°C.

Method

Knead the ingredients well
with the soaked grain meal.
Bulk fermentation approx.
60 minutes.

Working off

Hand up the dough pieces
lightly and eventually mould
tightly into round pieces. Well
dust the top surface with half-
white or rye flour, lightly press
out flat and place on boards.
After three quarter proof cut
through the pieces with a
torten divider, right to the
base and place on the oven
sets. After a short proof dock
the middle and place in a pre-
steamed medium hot oven.
When the loaves are set bake
out fully with an open damper.

Gupf bread

Dough

3 000 g water
  150 g yeast
  150 g Levit
  450 g skimmed milk powder
  120 g salt
2 700 g half-white flour
1 500 g whole wheat flour
  150 g oil

Dough temperature 22 to
24°C.

Method

Break down the yeast, Levit
and skimmed milk powder in
the water and then knead well
with the flour. Add the oil and
finally the salt.
Bulk fermentation 60 to
90 minutes.

Linseed bread

Working off

Weigh off the pieces and hand up round. After a short recovery, mould up again tightly. Turn the top surface in flour and place onto cloths with the closure underneath. After a proof of approx. 20 minutes completely press a ring through the piece. After a further proof of 5 to 10 minutes, lightly dock the centre, put in the oven with plenty of steam and bake out very thoroughly.

Dough

2800 g cold water
  140 g yeast
  120 g Levit
  100 g salt
1100 g dark flour
1100 g whole wheat flour
1100 g coarse whole rye meal
  500 g linseed

Dough temperature 22 to 24°C.

Method

Break down the yeast and Levit in cold water and then knead well with the flours. After three quarters of the kneading time add the salt and finally the linseed.
Bulk fermentation time 60 to 75 minutes.

Working off

Hand up the pieces lightly, then mould out long shapes and place in dusted baskets or directly onto sets. After a very good proof dock lightly and place in a steamed oven. Bake in a moderate heat and bake out the linseed bread with an open damper.

Corn (maize) bread

2 000 g corn (maize) middlings
2 700 g boiling hot water

Mix and allow to stand for at least 12 hours.

Sponge dough
(10 to 12 hours fermentation)

1 200 g water
15 g yeast
1 800 g half-white flour

Dough

3 000 g sponge dough
4 500 g corn (maize) grits
450 g water
150 g yeast
300 g sugar
150 g salt
2 200 g half-white flour
150 g butter
1 100 g sultanas

Dough temperature 22 to 24°C.

Method

Make a dough from the sponge, yeast, sugar and flour. After ⅔ of the mixing time add the maize middlings and knead intensively again. Then add the butter, the salt and the sultanas right at the end. Bulk fermentation approx. 60 minutes.

Working off

Hand the dough pieces round, allow to recover and then mould tightly. Place onto greased sheets and allow to prove. Before baking, allow to stand for a short while in a cold place, brush twice with egg and cut. Bake in a moderate oven without steam and with the damper open.

Potato bread

Dough

3 000 g water
250 g yeast
150 g Levit
150 g milk powder
150 g salt
2 250 g half-white flour
2 250 g dark flour
750 g mashed potatoes

Dough temperature 22 to 24°C.

Method

Break down the yeast, Levit and milk powder in the water and start to knead together with the flours. After 2 to 3 minutes add the mashed potatoes and finally the salt. Bulk fermentation approx. 60 minutes.

Working off

Weigh off the dough pieces, hand up round, rest for a short time. Mould out to long spindle shapes, roll the top surface in rye flour and place

Barley bread

with the closure uppermost on dough cloths. After a full proof make a diagonal cut on the top and place in a not-too-hot oven with steam. Bake in decreasing heat and bake out with the damper open.

Production with potato flakes

If potato flakes are used in place of the mashed potatoes, then extra liquid must also be added.
For this recipe use 250 g potato flakes and an extra 500 g water.

Dough

3 000 g water
  200 g yeast
  150 g Levit
  100 g salt
2 000 g barley whole meal
2 000 g dark flour

Dough temperature 22 to 24°C.

Method

Break down the yeast and Levit in cold water and start to knead into the previously mixed flours. Then add the salt and knead the dough further.
Bulk fermentation 60 minutes.

Working off

Hand up the dough pieces round and then pin out flat. Brush immediately with water, roll in barley flour and place on the oven sets. After a full proof cut with an upright blade once firmly across the centre. Bake in a hot oven with plenty of steam and when the loaves have set finish the baking with an open damper.

Rye meal bread

Rome bread

Sponge dough

1 000 g water
   50 g ferment
1 200 g whole rye meal, fine
     grained

Mix together and work well.
Sponge temperature 20 to
22°C.
Leave to lie for 4 hours.

Dough

2 200 g sponge dough
2 000 g water
  180 g yeast
  100 g salt
1 800 g coarse whole rye meal
2 000 g half-white flour

Dough temperature 26 to
28°C.

Method

Make a dough from the
sponge and the other ingredients.
Bulk fermentation approx.
60 minutes.

Working off

Weigh off pieces appropriate
to the basket size and mould
to the length needed. Work
carefully so that no blisters
form. After full proof place the
loaves in a well steamed
medium hot oven. Let the
steam out after a few minutes
to hinder any break along the
sides of the loaves.

Dough

3 000 g water
  150 g yeast
  150 g Levit
  100 g salt
1 500 g whole wheat flour, fine
3 000 g half-white flour
  300 g flake hazelnuts

Dough temperature 22 to
24°C.

Method

Mix all of the ingredients, with
the exception of the hazelnuts,
to a very well kneaded dough.
A light roasting of the hazelnuts will improve the flavour
of the bread. Add the nuts at
the end of the dough mixing.
Bulk fermentation time
approx. 60 minutes.

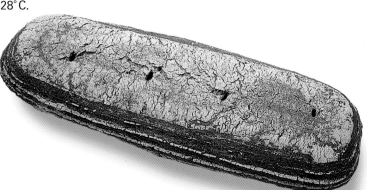

Nut bread

Working off

Mould the dough pieces round and allow to recover for 10 to 20 minutes. Press out flat and after a short proof press out twice crossways with the special stamp, to create eight equal pieces. Keep the proof short in order to achieve a clear marking. Brush the bread with water before putting in the oven and bake out well in a moderate oven.

Dough

2 000 g water
  200 g yeast
   40 g malt
  100 g salt
  200 g egg yolk
  500 g half-white flour
  500 g dark flour
  500 g rye flour, half white
  500 g coarse whole rye meal
1 000 g whole wheat flour
1 000 g walnuts, coarsely
         chopped
  400 g butter

Dough temperature 22 to 24°C.

Method

Mix the yeast and malt in the water and pre-mix with the flours. Stir the salt into the egg yolk and then add. At half of the kneading process add the butter and at the end of the kneading process the walnuts.
Bulk fermentation time approx. 60 minutes.

Working off

Weigh off the dough pieces, hand them up round and then work them to the long shapes. Place into the greased tins and prove well. Before baking brush the top surface with egg and make three long cuts with the blade. Place the articles in a presteamed mild oven. After about 30 minutes remove from the tins and finish baking with an open damper.

Wheat flake bread

Oatmeal bread

Dough

3000 g water
150 g yeast
120 g Levit
120 g salt
3500 g dark flour
750 g wheat flakes

Dough temperature 22 to 24°C.

Method

Break down the yeast and Levit in cold water and knead with the dark flour. Add the salt when threequarters mixed and the flakes right at the end of the kneading process. Bulk fermentation time 60 to 70 minutes.

Working off

Work out the dough pieces first to a long shape and then with the machine to long bands 2½ mm thick. Tightly roll up these bands as for the Mailand bread. After a good proof cut along the length in the middle to a good depth and place in a pre-steamed oven. Finish baking out quite well with the damper open.

Dough

3000 g water
200 g yeast
100 g Levit
100 g salt
3000 g dark flour
1000 g oatmeal

Dough temperature 22 to 24°C.

Method

Break down the yeast and Levit in water and knead well with the flour. After three quarters of the mixing time add the salt, and the oatmeal right at the end.
Bulk fermentation approx. 60 minutes

Working off

Hand the dough pieces up round first and then into long shapes. Brush the top surface with egg and roll in oatmeal. Place on cloths with the closure uppermost and tuck in. After full proof turn the loaves over onto oven sets and bake in a pre-steamed medium oven. When the loaves are set bake off with the damper open.

Bran bread

Dough

1 500 g water
600 g coarse bran

Mix and allow to stand for
90 minutes.

1 500 g water
250 g yeast
90 g Levit
90 g salt
1 000 g half-white flour
1 000 g dark flour
1 000 g whole wheat flour

Method

Knead the ingredients
together with the soaked bran
to form a dough. Do not add
the salt until about ¾ of the
way through the kneading
time.
Bulk fermentation time
60 minutes.

Working off

Weigh off the dough pieces
and first hand them up round
and eventually to longer
shapes. Brush the top surface
with egg, roll in bran and then
place on cloths or directly
onto setting slips. After a full
proof lightly dock the bread
and place in a pre-steamed
hot oven. When set bake out
with an open damper.

Sesame bread

Dough

3 000 g water
250 g yeast
150 g Levit
120 g salt
300 g oil
4 000 g half-white flour
600 g sesame seeds

Dough temperature 22 to
24°C.

Method

Break down the yeast and
Levit in cold water and knead
well with the flour. At half of
the kneading time add the oil,
the salt together with the
sesame seeds being added at
the end.
Bulk fermentation time
approx. 60 minutes.

Working off

First hand up the dough
pieces round and then mould
tightly to the baton shapes.
Brush with egg, roll in sesame
seeds and place on the oven
sets. After a full proof dock
lightly and place in a medium
hot oven with steam. After the
loaves have set bake off with
an open damper, fully but to a
light colour.

Rye bread

Rye bread with sour dough

Indirect fermentation process

Sponge dough

1 200 g water
   50 g ferment
1 800 g dark rye flour

Sponge temperature 26 to 28° C. Fermentation time 6 to 8 hours.

Dough

2500 g sponge dough
1 800 g water
  120 g yeast
  100 g salt
1 800 g dark rye flour
  900 g dark flour

Dough temperature 26 to 28° C.

Method

Knead the ingredients to a dough.
Bulk fermentation 40 to 60 minutes.

Working off

First hand up the weighed off dough pieces and then mould to batons. Place on to rye flour dusted boards with the closure uppermost. After a full proof mark with a blade and place in plenty of steam. After a few minutes let the steam out and finish baking.

Sponge dough

Fermentation time: 12 hours

1 000 g water
  50 g ferment
1 700 g dark rye flour

Sponge temperature 25 to 28° C.

Dough

2700 g sponge dough
2 000 g water, 20° C
  200 g yeast
  100 g salt
1 300 g dark rye flour
1 300 g dark wheat flour

Dough temperature 28 to 30° C.

Method

First break down the sponge in the water, then mix with the flour to a plastic dough, but do not knead too long.
Bulk fermentation 20 to 30 minutes.

Working off

Mould the dough pieces tightly and place on boards or in baskets. Before placing in the oven cut a diamond pattern in the top centre and dock well. Use plenty of steam at first, let the steam out after a few minutes and bake out well.

Rye caraway bread
with sour dough

Sponge dough

Fermentation time 10 to 12 hours

1 000 g water
100 g ferment
1 700 g rye flour, dark or half-white
100 g caraway seeds

Dough

2 900 g sponge dough
2 000 g water, 20°C
200 g yeast
100 g salt
1 400 g rye flour, dark or half-white
1 400 g dark flour

Dough temperature 26 to 28°C.

Method

Mix the sponge with the other ingredients but only knead for a short time (3 to 4 minutes in a fast mixer, 5 to 6 in an upright mixer).
Bulk fermentation time 50 to 60 minutes.

Working off

Hand up the dough pieces, allow to recover and then mould tightly. Roll in rye flour and enclose in cloths with the closure uppermost, or place in the special baskets. After full proof dock well and place in a fully warm oven with steam. After about 2 minutes open the damper and bake out fully.

Fruit bread

Dough

1000 g dark bread dough
1000 g whole wheat flour
  700 g water
  100 g yeast
  100 g sugar
   20 g salt
  200 g hazelnuts or raw
    almonds (whole or
    coarsely chopped)
  100 g sultanas
  100 g currants
  100 g dried prunes (soaked
    and stoned)
  100 g dried apple slices
  100 g orange-lemon peel

Method

Mix all of the ingredients, with the exception of the kernels and fruits, to a dough. Add the fruits at the end.
Bulk fermentation 60 minutes.

Working off

Hand up dough pieces to the required size and then mould out long. Place in greased tins and brush with egg. After full proof bake in a medium hot oven. When baked brush with starch wash or hot syrup.

Small breads
and
small articles

Small breads

Semmel, Schlumbergerli, Glarus small rolls, Double semmel, Pariserli

Dough

1 000 g water
60 g yeast
30 g Levit
20 g malt
40 g salt
1 800 g white flour, possibly
⅓ half-white flour,
⅔ white flour

Method

Knead the ingredients together with the exception of the salt. Add the salt at half time and then work the dough until well plasticised. Cover and allow to ferment for approx. 60 minutes without knocking back.

Express method

Dough

1 000 g water
125 g yeast
30 g Levit
20 g malt
40 g salt
1 200 g white flour
600 g half-white flour

Method

Knead the ingredients to a dough with the exception of the salt. Add the salt when half mixed. As the fermentation time for the Express semmel is reduced to a minimum the dough must be well kneaded. This means that it should be done in an upright or high speed mixer. Weigh off the pieces, mould up round and leave covered to prove for approx. 20 minutes.

SEMMEL

Weigh off the pieces in a divider and mould round. Place the rolls onto cloths or onto oven sets and cover with plastic. After about three quarters proving time remove the cover and allow to stand for a while. Before placing in the oven cut across the middle so that it creates the typical «cap». Put the rolls in a very hot oven previously steamed, after 10 minutes let the steam out and bake to a crisp crust.

SCHLUMBERGERLI

Weigh off pieces for the divider-moulder. Brush the plate of the machine with oil, press and lightly mould off. Place the rolls onto well flour dusted oven sets with the closure underneath. After a good proof turn them over and with the closure uppermost place in a pre-steamed quite hot oven. In this way the Schlumbergerli will open out nicely. In order to get a crisp crust remove the steam after approx. 10 minutes.

GLARUS SMALL ROLLS

Weigh off pieces of the
Semmel dough for the divider,
divide and first mould up
round. Eventually knock them
out slightly longer in shape
and place on cloths or setting
boards. Before baking cut at
an angle across the middle.
Place in a hot oven with steam
and then bake out with the
damper open.

DOUBLE SEMMEL

Weigh off pieces of the
Semmel dough for the divider,
divide and mould up round.
Put two rolls together, place
on cloths or sets and allow to
prove. Before baking cut
across both pieces lengthways
as for Semmel. Bake in a hot
oven with steam and bake out
with the damper open.

PARISERLI

Weigh off pieces of Semmel
dough at about 120 g, work off
to long shapes and place on
cloths or oven sets with the
closure uppermost. Turn over
while still under-proof and cut
twice. Bake in a hot oven and
bake out with the damper
open.

Farmer rolls

Rye rolls

Dough

- 500 g water
- 500 g milk
- 75 g yeast
- 50 g Levit
- 35 g salt
- 1 300 g farmer flour (70% dark flour, 30% rye flour)

Method

Work the ingredients to a dough. Keep the dough cold and knead well.
Bulk fermentation approx. 60 minutes.

Working off

Divide pieces in the machine and mould round. Place the dough pieces with the closure uppermost onto flour dusted boards and prove. Turn over when half proved so that the floury side is now uppermost. Before baking cut twice cross-ways and bake on the oven bottom in a hot oven with steam. The Farmer rolls must be given a strong crisp crust.

Dough

- 2 000 g water
- 80 g yeast
- 100 g Levit
- 60 g salt
- 950 g dark flour
- 1 850 g whole rye meal, fine grained

Method

Mix all ingredients together and knead. The kneading will take 6 to 8 minutes according to the type of mixer used.
Bulk fermentation 60 minutes.

Working off

Divide and mould the pieces round. Roll on all sides in rye flour, place with the closure underneath directly onto oven sets, or on cloths. Press out flat immediately and place to prove for 60 minutes. The correct proof will be seen by the even cracks which appear evenly all over the top surface. Place in a hot oven with steam. When set, bake off well with the damper open.

Graham rolls

Direct fermentation

Dough

2 000 g water
   40 g yeast
  100 g Levit
   10 g malt
   60 g salt
2 800 g whole wheat meal, fine
       grained

Dough temperature 22 to 24°C.
Bulk fermentation 180 minutes.

Indirect fermentation

Sponge dough

1 500 g water
   10 g yeast
2 000 g whole wheat meal, fine
       grained

Dough

  500 g water
   60 g yeast
   10 g malt
   60 g salt
  800 g whole wheat meal, fine
       grained

Method

Knead the sponge dough well
and allow to ferment for 6 to
8 hours. Then mix to a well
kneaded dough with the
remaining ingredients.
Bulk fermentation approx.
90—120 minutes.

Working off

Divide pieces, hand up round
and then to longer shapes.
Prove fully and bake with
steam in a very hot oven.
After baking brush immediately with water or a starch
wash.

St. Gallen Bürli

Indirect fermentation

Sponge dough

1 000 g water
1 300 g half-white flour
50 g yeast

Ferment 3 to 4 hours.

Dough

2 300 g sponge dough
2 000 g water
2 200 g half-white flour
50 g yeast
90 g salt

Method

Work the sponge into the water and then knead to a dough with the other ingredients. The dough should be very soft, but dry and stable. Fermentation time 1 to 1½ hours, knocking back three times during that time.

Working off

Break off dough pieces by hand directly from the ripe, plastic, bulk dough. Do not mould these but rather press them lightly together and then put two to four of them onto dusted boards. After a good proof put in a quite hot oven with plenty of steam. When they are set open the damper slightly. The Bürli must be well baked out and have a quite thick floury crust.

Salt weggen

Sponge dough

Fermentation time: 1 hour

500 g water
30 g yeast
800 g white flour

Dough

1300 g sponge dough
500 g water
50 g yeast
20 g malt
40 g salt
1 100 g white flour

The dough can also be made by the straight dough method instead of the ferment and dough system.

Method

As for Semmel dough.

Working off

Pre-mould dough pieces of approx. 60 g. After a short recovery time press the edge flat all around so that a raised portion is left in the middle. Turn the edge, which should be about 2 cm wide, in even portions 8 to 10 times inwards. Place the Salt weggen upside down on cloths to prove. Turn over before baking, brush with egg and sprinkle with caraway and salt. Bake in a hot oven with steam and finally bake off with an open damper.

Poppyseed rolls, poppyseed roses, poppyseed weggli, Prag points

Dough

1 000 g water
   80 g yeast
   30 g Levit
   20 g malt
   40 g salt
1 850 g white flour

To refine the dough 1 dl oil can be added, or milk can be used in place of the water.

Method

As for Semmel dough.

POPPYSEED ROLLS

Weigh off pieces for the divider and leave to prove for approx. 20 minutes. Then divide, mould round and brush the top surface with egg. Dip in poppyseed, place on cloths and prove. Just before they are fully proved allow to stand for a short time in a cooler place. Using a pair of scissors cut at an angle four times so that four points are formed. Then cut another four times around the sides and put in a pre-steamed quite hot oven, and finish baking out with the damper open.

POPPYSEED ROSES

After moulding the dough pieces round allow them to prove a short time, lightly dust with rye flour and then press out with a Kaiser roll cutter. Brush with egg, dip in poppy-seeds and allow to prove fully. Bake in pre-steamed hot oven and bake out fully.

POPPYSEED WEGGLI

Mould the dough pieces round
and then half long shapes.
Brush with egg and dip in
poppyseeds. Place on cloths
and after about three-quarters
proof time allow to stand in a
cool place for a short time.
Cut with a sharp knife. Bake in
a pre-steamed hot oven and
then bake out fully with the
damper open.

PRAG POINTS

Mould the dough pieces round
and after a short recovery roll
them out oval and finally roll
up to crescent types. Brush
the rolled-up pieces with egg
and then dip them into poppy-
seeds. Place onto sheets and
give the maximum proof so
that they will not burst open
as they are being baked. Bake
in a pre-steamed hot oven and
bake out with an open
damper.

Cornetti, Mailand rolls, Fingers

Dough

1 000 g water
    80 g yeast
    30 g Levit
    20 g malt
    50 g salt
2 000 g white flour
  100 g oil

Method

Break down the yeast, Levit
and malt in the water and
knead with the flour. Half way
through the kneading time
add the oil and the salt at the
end, and finish kneading.
Dough fermentation 20 to
30 minutes.

CORNETTI

Put 1500 g of dough in the 30
piece divider, pin out in the
crescent machine, dust all
over with rye flour and allow
to recover, covered, for about
10 minutes. Now halve them
and again pass them through
the crescent machine. The
second rolling gives a finer
and larger Cornetti. Place in
pairs to the Cornetti shape
and place on cloths or directly
onto setting boards. Bake in a
moderate oven in steam and
bake out with the damper
open. Do not wash the Cornetti. They should rather have
a slightly floury, crisp but light
coloured crust.

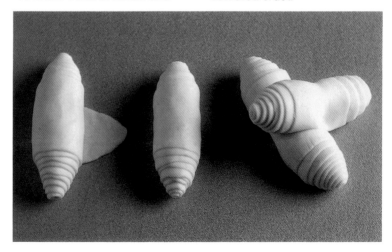

MAILAND ROLLS

Weigh off pieces from the Cornetti dough at 60 to 80 g and mould out long. After a short rest pin out these pieces to a long band and, using a machine, or by hand, roll up tightly from the one side. The spiral must be visible when this is complete. Allow the pieces to prove well and before baking cut deeply lengthways on top. Bake in a moderate oven with steam and finish baking out

with an open damper crisp and crusty, but with a light colour.

FINGERS

Work off Cornetti dough in a similar manner to Cornetti. Roll up the dough strip evenly from both sides, and using the hand or a round wooden stick press down in the middle of the parallel lying rolls. Press two parts lightly out of each other on one side and then twist the two opposite parts over each other, by turning them around. Place on cloths or directly onto the oven sets and turn over when fully

proved. Bake on the oven bottom in a mild oven with steam and finish baking out to a crust but pale colour, with the damper open.

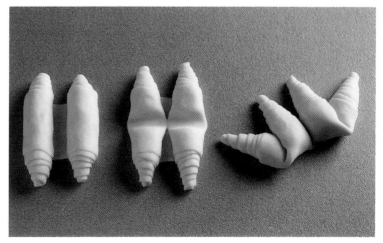

Small articles

Weggli, Cut Weggli, Sandwich or Ham rolls, Weggli crescents

Dough (Express method)

1 000 g milk
  125 g yeast
   30 g Levit
   20 g malt
   20 g sugar
   40 g salt
  200 g butter
1 800 g white flour, possibly
     ⅓ half-white flour,
     ⅔ white flour

Method

Mix the ingredients to a dough with the exception of the butter and salt. Add the butter only when the dough is well kneaded and the salt right at the end of the mixing process.

WEGGLI

Weigh the dough into pieces for the divider as soon as it is mixed and allow to recover for 20 to 30 minutes. Eventually divide, mould round and place the pieces directly onto greased sheets. Press the Weggli out with only a little proof. Eventually allow to rest for a short time in a cooler place. Then brush with egg and allow to prove further. Bake in a moderate oven without steam. After 2 to 3 minutes pipe steam into the oven and finish baking off to a light colour with an open damper.

CUT WEGGLI

Divide Weggli dough and mould round. Eventually mould out long fingers, place onto greased sheets and allow to prove a little. While still underproved place in a cooler place, then brush with egg and cut with the scissors down the length, an in and out running pattern. Bake as for the normal Weggli.

SANDWICH OR HAM ROLLS

Weigh off pieces of Weggli dough at 80 to 120 g and first mould up round. After a short recovery time mould out to long spindle shapes and place directly onto greased sheets. Press out flatter while under-proved, then brush with egg and allow full proof. Bake in a moderate oven without steam for 2 or 3 minutes, then add steam and finally bake out fully with an open damper to a light colour.

Brioches

WEGGLI CRESCENTS

Weigh off pieces for the divider as soon as the dough is mixed and allow to recover for 20 to 30 minutes. Then pin out to flat discs, dust all over with rye flour and form to crescent lengths in the machine. Before baking, brush with egg and allow to dry out for a short time. Place in the oven without steam. After 2 to 3 minutes steam and bake out to a light colour with the damper open.

Dough

100 g	milk
100 g	yeast
20 g	malt
100 g	sugar
25 g	salt
400 g	eggs
1 000 g	white flour
300 g	butter

Method

Break down the yeast, malt and sugar in the milk and mix with the flour. Stir the salt into the egg and add at 2 to 3 intervals. Add the butter only when the dough is well formed. Then knead the dough well and allow to stand for approx. 6 to 8 hours in a cool place.

Working off

Mould the weighed pieces (35 to 40 g) round and allow to recover. The head piece should be formed from about $\frac{1}{4}$ to $\frac{1}{3}$ of the whole dough piece. This should be rolled with the back of the hand so that the head is separated from the rest of the dough and held together only by a very thin strand. Place the bottom part in a well greased fluted tin and press right down in the middle so that the head can be placed into this depression. Put the brioches to prove, then stand in a cool place and carefully brush twice with egg. Bake in a hot oven with open damper to a fine light brown colour.

It is an advantage if the Brioches are put on a hot sheet to bake so that they set off quicker and break open better. As the dough contains a lot of egg the Brioches should be baked quickly so that they do not dry out too much.

The dough can be made in advance and kept in the deep freeze until needed.

Fastenwähen

(Carnival bread)

Sponge dough

500 g milk
60 g yeast
700 g white flour

Dough

1 200 g sponge dough
500 g milk
20 g malt
40 g salt
1 000 g white flour
600 g butter

Method

Put the ferment in a cool place for approx. 3 hours to ferment. Break down the salt and malt in the cold milk, break the ripe ferment into it and then mix to a fine dough with the flour. Add the butter only when the dough has been fully created.
Allow the dough to recover for 1 hour in the fridge.

Working off

Weigh off dough pieces at 40 to 50 g, mould round first and then to a spindle shape. Make both ends fairly pointed and ensure that the closure line is straight and lies underneath. Place these moulded pieces on well dusted cloths and leave to prove. When barely proved allow to stand in a cold place. Before they are fully set press in lightly with the back of the hand down the length and place them on a clean undusted board. Press out with the special cutter, brush twice with egg and sprinkle with caraway. Eventually pull apart to create a square and place on sheets. The breads can also be baked on the oven bottom. Bake in a hot oven with the damper open and no steam, for a short bake to a crispy crust.

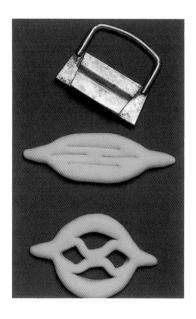

Sweet enriched fermented goods, made from sweet yeast dough (filled and unfilled)

Sweet yeast dough

Sugar rolls   Kreuzli

Dough

1 000 g milk
  150 g yeast
   30 g Levit
   20 g malt
  200 g sugar
   40 g salt
  100 g eggs
2 000 g white flour
      lemon, vanilla
  200 g butter

Method

Break down the yeast, Levit, malt and sugar in the milk and mix with the flour. Stir the salt into the egg and add. Finally add the butter and knead the dough well.
Bulk fermentation 1 to 1½ hours in a cool place.

Divide and mould round. Place on greased sheets. After threequarter proof brush twice with egg and sprinkle with nib sugar. Bake in a moderate oven without steam.

Weigh off pieces of sweet dough at approx. 50 g and mould out long. After a short recovery roll out to approx. 25 cm long and 5 cm wide. Brush with warm butter, sprinkle with a little sugar and a few sultanas spread over the top. Roll up the dough strips and cut into two down the length. Place across each other with the cut uppermost onto sheets and allow to prove. Before baking brush with egg and bake in a mild pre-steamed oven. After baking brush with apricot, glaze and decorate with flake almonds and nib sugar.

Little twisted plait

Prepare dough pieces as for the Kreuzli. Roll out and cut, then plait in each other and twist up. After glazing sprinkle with nib sugar.

Creme spirals

Pin out sweet yeast dough to a rectangle 2 mm thick and first cover with hazelnut filling and then spread a little vanilla creme over that. Sprinkle on a few currants or sultanas and roll up the whole piece. The completed roll should only be approx. 5 cm thick. From the roll now cut pieces about 4 cm wide, press these out from the middle with a stick and place on greased sheets or silicon paper. After a good proof brush with egg and bake in a moderate oven with steam. Finally apricot and glaze.

Creme rolls

Prepare dough pieces as for Kreuzli, spread with vanilla creme and roll up. Place the pieces on sheets and cut deeply down to the bottom along the centre, lengthways, with scissors. After three-quarter proof brush with egg and bake in a moderate oven with steam. Finally apricot and glaze.

Appenzell nut summits

Pin out the desired weight of dough 2½ mm thick and after a short recovery cut into rectangles of 8 × 15 cm. Along the centre, pipe as much brown filling (hazelnut filling) as there is dough. Fold both sides over the length and place the summits with the closure underneath, either straight or slightly curved, onto sheets. Press lightly flat and leave to prove. When fully proved brush with egg, lightly dock and bake in a moderate oven with steam. Brush the summits with melted butter while they are hot, allow to go cold and then roll in sugar.

Plaited sweet yeast dough goods

Small single strand plait

Golatsch

For plaited sweet yeast dough articles it is an advantage to keep the dough fairly tight. Fermentation 30 minutes. Place the worked up pieces on sheets and leave to prove. After threequarters proof brush with egg and bake in a moderate oven with the damper open.

Roll out dough pieces evenly to 40 cm long strands. Shape each strand to a bow with one longer end. Pull the long piece once through underneath, turn the bow over and pull the end through from below.

Roll out dough pieces evenly as for the single strand plait. Press both ends together and with the closure underneath, set on sheets.

Cinnamon buttons

Roll out dough pieces in cinnamon sugar to long strands, with the ends slightly thicker than the middle. Plait these to a button shape, place on sheets and allow to prove. Bake in a moderate oven with the damper open. The sugar will lightly caramelise on the bottom as baking takes place.

Tie buttons

Roll out a dough length of approx. 35 cm and place in a U shape with the ends underneath on the table. Turn the U part over and pull both ends through the opening thus created.

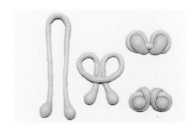

Scissors

Roll out a piece of dough to a strand approx. 35 cm long, form to a U shape and place on the table with the ends underneath. Turn the U part over and the two ends through, the bow thus formed are then twisted outwards once.

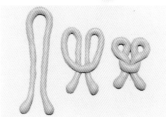

Corkscrew

Roll out a dough strand and twist the middle part into a three part bow. Twist the two ends together into each other.

Sweet «S» or Spectacles

Pipes

Rosettes

Roll up a length of dough from both ends and form to an «S» or pair of spectacles.

Shape a length of dough to look like a pipe.

Dough

1 000 g	milk
150 g	yeast
30 g	Levit
20 g	malt
200 g	sugar
40 g	salt
	lemon and vanilla
1 900 g	white flour
200 g	butter
300 g	sultanas

Method

Break down the yeast, Levit, malt and sugar in the milk and knead with the flour to a dough. Add the butter to the well worked dough, followed by the salt and the washed and dried sultanas at the end as carefully as possible. Bulk fermentation time 1 to 1½ hours.

Working off

Weigh off pieces of dough at approx. 50 g and mould out to long shapes. Allow to recover, then roll out to small strips of approx. 25 cm length. Brush these dough strips with melted butter, sprinkle with sugar and make cuts in one long side at 1 cm intervals, up to the middle. Roll up the strips formed by the cuts and place on greased sheets. With full proof bake in a hot oven with steam. While still hot brush with melted butter, and when cold roll in sugar.

Small almond rolls

Dough

As for Rosettes but in place of
300 g sultanas:
150 g chopped orange-lemon
　　peel
100 g ground blanched almonds
150 g sultanas
　　fiori di Sicillia, lemon

Working off

Weigh off dough pieces at
80 to 100 g, mould round and
place on cloths. With medium
proof handle as Weggli,
marking out with the cross
twice over each other. Brush
with egg and dip into a
mixture of ½ fine flake white
almonds and ½ sugar. Place
the almond rolls onto greased
sheets and finish proving.
With full proof bake in a
moderate oven with steam.
The sugar in the mixture will
caramelise lightly during the
baking.

Kapuziner rolls

Dough

1 000 g	milk
100 g	yeast
30 g	Levit
10 g	malt
200 g	sugar
40 g	salt
200 g	eggs
1 850 g	white flour
200 g	butter
	lemon zest
300 g	sultanas

Method

Break down the yeast, Levit,
malt and sugar in the milk and
mix with the flour to a dough.
Mix the salt in the egg and
slowly add to the dough.
When half kneaded add the
butter and finally the washed
and dried sultanas. Allow the
dough to stand in a cool place
for approx. 1 hour.

Working off

Weigh off dough pieces of
50 to 60 g, mould round and
place onto greased sheets.
With moderate proof, brush
twice with egg. Pin out sweet
paste to 2 to 3 mm thick, cut
out 6 cm diameter pieces with
a plain cutter and place these
on the dough pieces. After a
further short proof bake in a
moderate oven with open
damper to a light colour.

Meitschibei

Nut sticks

Dough

1 500 g white flour
400 g butter
500 g milk
50 g yeast
150 g sugar
10 g malt
20 g salt
100 g eggs

Method

Mix the flour and butter together and knead to a dough with the rest of the ingredients until all is plastic. Leave in a cool place to ferment.

Filling

1 500 g lightly roast ground hazelnuts
750 g sugar
200 g glucose
100 g butter
20 g cinnamon
300 g water, approx.

Method

Mix all of the ingredients together and mill to a fine but tight mixture. This should have a similar consistency to that of the dough.

Working off

Pin out the dough to 1¾ mm thick. Cut out discs of 18 × 7 cm and brush with egg. Take 30 g of the filling per Meitschibei and roll it out also to 18 cm long and carefully enclose it in the dough. Roll out to sticks of 22 cm long and place on greased sheets in the desired shape. Before baking brush twice with egg and bake in a hot oven without steam.

Dough and filling as for the Meitschibei.

Working off

Pin out the dough to 1¾ mm thick, cut out to 14 × 7 cm and brush with egg. Take 30 g of filling per nut stick and roll it out to 14 cm long. Place on the base and roll up carefully. Roll out to sticks of 18 cm long and place straight out onto sheets. Before baking brush twice with egg and bake in a hot oven without steam.

Small articles made from laminated doughs

Paris crescents

Dough

1 000 g milk
100 g yeast
20 g Levit
20 g malt
40 g sugar
50 g salt
150 g eggs
2 000 g white flour
100 g butter

700 g butter, crescent fat or
puff pastry margarine
for enclosing

Method

Break down the yeast, Levit, malt and sugar in the very cold milk and mix with the flour. Stir the salt into the egg and add. Add the butter when it is half kneaded and finish the kneading process. Pin out the dough to a rectangle, place on a sheet and cover it with a sheet of plastic and allow it to stand in the fridge for approx. 60 minutes. Then enclose the butter and give three single turns at intervals. Do not pin out thinner than 10 mm so that the butter layers are kept in place. Allow the dough to stand in the fridge overnight. See that the dough doesn't collapse by the next morning.
This dough is also good for a fermentation period of only 1 to 2 hours. In this case the yeast is raised to 150 g per liter.

Working off

Pin out dough pieces approx. 2,5 mm thick and with the roller or a knife cut out triangles of 35 to 40 g each. Carefully roll these up to crescents with the machine and place on sheets. Prove in the bakery covered with a cloth, or in a not-too-warm prover (28 to 30° C). Brush with egg before baking, allow to dry out a little and then bake in a hot oven with steam to start. Bake out well with the damper open.

Whole wheat crescents

Dough

1 000 g water
100 g yeast
50 g Levit
10 g malt
20 g sugar
50 g Tourit
40 g salt
150 g eggs
1 600 g whole wheat flour, extra fine *
700 g butter, crescent margarine or crescent fat for enclosing

* Grain size for an extra fine whole wheat flour is smaller than 0,5 mm.

Croissants feuilletés

(French method)

Method

Dissolve the malt and sugar in the water and mix with all the ingredients except the salt and the eggs. Stir the salt into the eggs and knead the dough carefully.
Bulk fermentation: 60 minutes

Turning

Pin out the dough to a rectangle, place on a baking tray and cover with plastic. Allow it to stand in the freezer for about 45 minutes. Enclose the fat on 2/3 of the dough and give in short intervals three single turns of 10 mm. Let the dough to prove in the refrigerator for 3—4 hours.

Working off

Pin out the dough 5$^{1}/_{2}$—6 mm thick and cut with a triangular roller 12 cm wide and 10,5 cm high (ca. 45 g). Using the machine, roll the dough pieces up to crescents and place on a baking tray. Cover with plastic and allow to prove at room temperature. Bake in a middle warm oven with steam. Finish baking with the damper open.

Dough

1 000 g water, cold
    50 g yeast (in winter 70 g)
    40 g malt
    60 g milk powder
    80 g sugar
    40 g salt
1 800 g white flour

   600 g butter to be enclosed

Method

Break down all of the ingredients in the water and work to a dough with the flour. Knead well and then allow to ferment in a cool place for 4 to 5 hours. Enclose the butter and give 3 single turns at short intervals. Allow the turned dough to lie in the fridge for approx. 1 hour.

Working off

Pin out the dough to about 3 mm thick and with a roller or a knife cut out the triangles. Carefully roll these up to crescents with a machine or by hand without using any force, and place on sheets. Place in a cool prover (28 to 30° C) or prove in the bakery temperature covered with a cloth. Brush with egg before baking, allow to dry off for a short time and bake in a pre-steamed oven; baking out well with the damper open.

Sweet enriched fermented goods, made from laminated sweet yeast dough

Nut crescents, Spirals

Laminated sweet yeast dough

1 000 g milk
150 g yeast
20 g malt
200 g sugar
40 g salt
100 g eggs
     lemon zest
100 g butter
2 000 g white flour

600 g butter or puff pastry margarine to be enclosed

Method

Break down the yeast, malt and sugar in the cold milk and mix with the flour. Stir the salt and lemon zest in the egg and add. Finally add the butter and knead well.
Pin out the dough to a rectangle and divide the plasticised butter over $^2/_3$ of the surface and enclose. Give three single turns at intervals of 10 to 15 minutes. It can then be worked off after a rest of a further 30 to 50 minutes or left covered overnight in a cool place (in this case only use 100 g yeast per liter).

NUT CRESCENTS

Pin out the dough 2,5 mm thick and cut into triangles. Spread or pipe on hazelnut filling and roll the pieces up. Place onto sheets with the ends slightly turned in and prove in a not-too-warm place. When fully proved brush the nut crescents with egg, dock lightly and bake in a pre-steamed cool oven. Finally apricot and glaze. Possibly sprinkle a little flaked almond in the middle.

SPIRALS

Pin out laminated sweet yeast dough to about 2,5 mm thick, cut into a rectangle (approx. 45 cm wide), and cover with hazelnut filling. Roll up and cut pieces of the desired size (40 to 60 g). Place the spirals onto greased sheets or in foil moulds of 9 cm diameter, press out lightly and prove in a not-too-warm place. Before baking brush the spirals with egg and bake with steam in a moderate oven. Eventually apricot and glaze.

Danish pastries

Brezel, Schlüferli, Kämme, Gipfeli, Spandauer

Dough

1 000 g cold milk
200 g yeast
20 g malt
200 g sugar
40 g salt
250 g eggs
15 g cardamon powder
    lemon zest
100 g butter
2 200 g white flour
1 200 g butter of puff pastry
    margarine to be
    enclosed

Method

Break down the yeast, malt, sugar, spice and lemon in the cold milk and mix with the flour. Stir the salt into the egg and add. Then add the butter and knead the dough well. Roll this dough to a rectangle, spread the butter evenly over ²/₃ of the dough surface and enclose it. Give 3 single turns at intervals of 5 to 10 minutes. Keep the dough as cold as possible. Before working it off allow it to stand for at least ½ hour in a cold place. If possible work it off in a cold room too.

Working off

Do not roll any Danish pastry dough thinner than 3 mm. Do not prove the finished dough pieces in a too warm place, otherwise the butter will flow out. In order to keep the layers, only prove slowly at room temperature.

Fillings

Brown Danish filling:

1 000 g ground, lightly roast hazelnuts	finely milled
800 g sugar	
200 g glucose	
10 g cinnamon	
500 g water	

The mixture should be capable of being spread but not kept too soft.

White Danish filling:

500 g almonds	finely milled
500 g sugar	
200 g egg whites	

Thin the mixture to a spreading consistency with egg white or water and flavour with lemon.

Butter filling:

250 g raw sugar	cream together
250 g butter	

BREZEL

Pin out dough pieces of 25 to 30 cm wide. Spread half with white Danish filling and fold the other half over. Now cut strips 1 cm wide, twist these to the outside and form to Brezels. Allow to prove well and eventually brush with egg. After baking apricot and glaze.

SCHLÜFERLI

Pin out dough strips to 20 cm wide. Spread along the length of the centre a little baking jam and spread over it some of the butter filling. Place both long sides over the centre. With the closure uppermost cut into strips of 3 to 4 cm wide. Cut these pieces through the middle down the length. Pull one of the ends through this last cut, place on a sheets lined with silicon paper and prove. Before baking, brush the Schlüferli with egg and pipe vanilla creme in the centre. Bake in a moderate oven with steam. While still hot, brush with apricot and glaze.

KÄMME (Combs)

Pin out dough strips of 25 cm wide. Pipe brown filling first and butter filling over the top, down the length of the centre. Enclose as for the Schlüferli, brush the top with egg and sprinkle with flake hazelnuts. From this now cut strips 3 to 4 cm wide and then cut 5 or 6 notches down the one long side. Place the pieces in half-moon shapes onto sheets, prove and bake in a moderate oven. After baking, dust with icing sugar.

GIPFELI

Pin out a strip of dough to 24 cm wide. From this cut long triangles, pipe a little white almond filling in the middle and roll up to crescents. Place these on sheets and prove. Then brush with egg and bake in a moderate oven. Apricot and glaze while still hot. Sprinkle a few flake almonds on top.

SPANDAUER

Pin out the dough and cut squares of 10 × 10 cm. Pipe a bulb of white almond mixture in the centre. Place all four corners over to the centre and press down well. Place on sheets and prove. Bake in a moderate oven and while still hot, apricot and glaze the pieces.

Deep fried goods

Berlin Pancakes

(Doughnuts)

Dough

1000 g	milk
200 g	yeast
150 g	sugar
500 g	egg yolk
40 g	salt
	lemon zest
300 g	butter
2 100 g	white flour

Method

Break down the yeast and sugar in the milk and mix to a dough with the flour. Mix the egg yolk and salt and add a little at a time and finally add the butter. Knead the dough well until it is very fine and dry. Allow to ferment for 60—75 minutes.

Working off

Weigh off for the divider and mould round. Place on cloths and prove. With medium proof bake in hot fat at 180 to 200°C. While the pancakes are baking, turn them over two or three times so that they bake slowly and evenly. While still hot fill with raspberry jam and turn in cinnamon sugar. Finally possibly dust with icing sugar.

Variation

Fill the pancakes before baking. To do this mould the dough pieces round, allow to recover and then flatten them out. Pipe a little raspberry jam in the centre. Carefully close the dough pieces and place on cloths with the closure underneath. Bake when they have reached a medium proof.

Dough

300 g	milk
60 g	yeast
20 g	Levit
10 g	malt
10 g	salt
100 g	eggs
150 g	almond mixture
80 g	butter
	lemon zest
850 g	white flour
150 g	finely chopped candied fruits
1 500 g	puff pastry, prepared up to the second turn

124

Zürich-Zigerkrapfen

Method

Break down the yeast, Levit and malt in the milk and mix with the flour. Mix together the salt and eggs and add. Then add the butter and finally the almond mixture with the fruit being gently folded through. Allow the dough to ferment for approx. 30 minutes. Pin out the puff pastry to a rectangle, place the yeast dough on top and enclose it. Give three single turns with short intervals between each one.

Working off

Pin out 1,5 kg dough to 50 × 60 cm. From this now cut rectangles 5 × 10 cm. In the centre of each piece make a cut approx. 6 cm long. Pull one end through this cut, place on cloths and allow to prove. Bake in hot fat 180 to 200°C to a fine brown colour and finally roll in cinnamon sugar.

Dough

1 000 g Weggli dough
1 000 g puff pastry

Filling

1 000 g Ziger or curd cheese
  600 g almond mixture
finely milled together

  400 g vanilla creme
   50 g egg yolk
  100 g cream
  200 g sultanas
       a little Kirsch
       lemon zest
all added

Method

Place the yeast dough and puff pastry on top of each other and give three single turns before resting in a cool place for about half an hour. Then pin out the dough to 1,5 mm thick, cut out round discs (10 cm diam.) and pipe a bulb of filling in the centre. Brush the edges with egg and fold over as a turnover, pressing firmly together with the back of a cutter. Dock with a fork before baking. Bake and then roll in cinnamon sugar. Fat temperature: 200°C approx.

Caustic Soda rolls

Dough

1 000 g water
   80 g yeast
   20 g malt
   40 g salt
  100 g oil
2 000 g white flour

Method

Mix the dough ingredients to a dough without the oil and salt. After threequarters of the kneading time add the oil, followed by the salt.
Bulk fermentation time 15 to 20 minutes.

Caustic soda water solution

a) in trade offer:
Caustic soda solution below 5% strength is available ready for use and without poison certificate (max. 4,9%).

b) ones own preparation of the soda solution:
1 000 g warm water
   50 g Sodium hydroxide, pure, sold in discs
Boil the water and sodium hydroxide discs together until the discs are completely dissolved.

Temperature of use approx. 40°C.

BIERBREZEL (Beer pretzels)

Divide 1800 g dough into 30 pieces and mould out long. After a short rest roll out the pieces to strands of 45 to 50 cm long, leaving them thicker in the middle, then thinner and again slightly thicker at both ends. Form to Brezel, allow to prove slightly and eventually allow to stand in a cold place. Before baking, dip into the caustic soda solution, sprinkle with coarse salt and place in a not too hot oven on wires, or tefal sheets to bake out without steam.

SILSERBREZEL (Filled Brezel)

Divide 1500 g dough into
30 pieces and mould out long.
After a short recovery roll out
to 30 cm long even strands
and form into Brezel. Allow
these to prove a little and then
place in a cool place. Before
baking, dip in the caustic soda
solution, place on wires or
tefal sheets and sprinkle with
coarse salt. Bake in a
moderate oven with an open
damper. When they are cold,
cut in two through the middle
and fill with light creamed,
salted butter.

Butter filling

200 g butter
 40 g water
      salt

cream together

DELICE

Divide 1200 g of dough into
30 pieces and mould round.
Then mould out longer or
work off the pieces with the
machine to finger rolls. After a
short proof, stand in the fridge
for a short while, dip in the
caustic soda solution and
place on wires or teflon sheets
with the closure underneath.
Cut lightly down the length,
sprinkle with coarse salt and
bake in a mild oven without
steam. When cold cut open
and spread the inside with
creamed salted butter.

Butter filling

200 g butter
 40 g water
  5 g mustard
      salt

cream together

Variant

For a change the Silserbrezeli
or the Delice can be filled with
Coppa, Salami, Ham or cheese
slices.

Large yeast goods

Guide lines for the production of enriched yeast doughs

Handling enriched yeast dough

The richness of various yeast doughs is measured by the special higher quantities of ingredients such as butter, eggs and sugar. Over and above these there are a number of well-known pastries of sweet yeast dough with very high additions of fruits and kernels.
The trouble-free preparation of such doughs, to achieve a fine end product, the craftsman needs plenty of skill and knowledge. This demand is in the areas of dough manufacture, fermentation, working off and baking.

Sections

According to the ingredients, the doughs and other pastries can be placed in the following categories:

a) Doughs with high proportion of butter and eggs.
b) Doughs enriched with additions of fruits.
c) Enriched doughs with high additions of fruits and kernels.

The dough preparation

Basically all enriched yeast doughs need an intensive kneading of the ingredients before the addition of the butter or fruits.
This leads to an optimum creation of gluten with the corresponding firmness of dough. In this way it is able to enclose larger quantities of fruits and nuts and at the same time able to hold them in an even crumb.

The ingredients and their handling

Liquid content

For the majority of doughs milk is used as the liquid. This may be replaced by water in a long ferment because milk might go sour over the longer time.
According to the climate, richness of the recipe and the kneading system the liquid must be used cold with a temperature of 22 to 24°C being the aim. This then may possibly call for a temperature of the liquid which may vary between cold (10 to 12°C) down to fridge temperature (3 to 5°C) and cooled with ice.

Yeast

The yeast quantity is based on the richness and the fermentation method of the dough. According to the weight of the other ingredients it can be up to 3% to 10% of the flour quantity.

Salt

Rich yeast doughs require a higher quantity of salt than normal white flour doughs. The reason being that salt addition is calculated per liter of fluids and rich doughs produce a particularly large yield per liter. However the addition must not exceed 50 g per liter.

Sugar

The higher the proportion of sugar, the more it is necessary to ensure that it is fully dissolved in the liquid. Otherwise the doughs will be damp and sticky because of the undissolved portions. This then also leads to insufficient volume when baked. Doughs with higher sugar content need a longer mixing time to achieve the best results from the baking process.

Eggs

These are lightly mixed with the salt, and with larger quantities being used are added a little at a time, with the other ingredients. This method leads to a longer gluten, and consequently a longer dough structure. It gives a finer and smoother dough, which then helps with the baked volume.

Butter

The butter should be used in a cool, but smooth condition. It must not be greasy however. With very high quantities, as for Dresden Stollen for example, it is necessary to add it a little at a time. The addition of the butter should only occur when the dough is already kneaded to a dry and plastic consistency, so that the take-up of the food for the yeast and the development of the gluten is not obstructed.

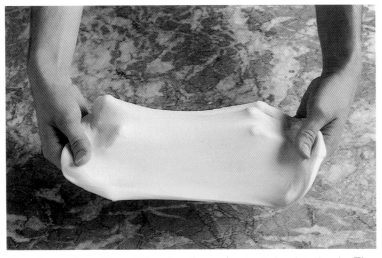

The stage of working of the dough can be tested quite simply. The picture shows the long, homogenous structure of a paper-thin drawn out piece of dough, without this tearing in the process.

Fruits and nuts

Fruits such as currants, sultanas and raisins should always be washed in cold water the day before and then soaked for 1 to 2 hours in water or alcohol (e. g. seed-fruit brandy, rum, etc.). Following this it should be left to drain on a sieve and dried on silicon paper. Before the addition, in order to enable it to be incorporated in the dough more easily, it can be lightly dusted with flour.

Candied fruits are mostly used in the diced condition. In this state there is the danger that the sharp edged dice may not work to an advantage on the dough. If the candied fruit is too hard it can be soaked previously to advantage in cold water and eventually dried. Warm water would be too likely to dissolve too much of the preservative sugar from the fruits.

Nuts should not be too finely chopped before use as otherwise it may not have sufficient effect.

The addition of fruits and nuts should only be done at the end of the kneading process. It also needs careful adding in the way it is mixed, until the fruits are evenly distributed throughout the dough.

Fermentation

The indirect fermentation process

With rich doughs there are many grounds for the use of a sponge or ferment.
- Better construction and development of the gluten. This gives with it a raising of the stability of the dough and a better stability of the crumb, in order to take up the larger quantities of butter, sugar and fruits.
- Increase of the creation of lactic and acetic acids as a cause for a longer fresh-keeping property which is brought about especially by a long fermentation period overnight.
- With a long fermentation period there is a greater creation of fermentation acids which give flavour and aroma.

The various high quantities of the different ingredients call for special indirect fermentation methods. The main systems are the long sponge overnight, the shorter sponge, the quick ferment and the Pouliche.
- The longe sponge system serves especially well for the two yeast articles of Panettoni and Gugelhopf. The long lying time brings in the first line an improvement in the taste and at the same time a good effect on the keeping qualities of freshness.
- The short sponge is often used for the Easter Dove and such types of baked goods.
- A quick ferment serves in the very heavy Dresden Stollen to hydrate the gluten. In this way it gives a better plastic dough, which will show itself in the better volume.
- The Pouliche as an extremely soft ferment offers especially the so-called long dough structure and brings a higher moistness to the end product. The Pouliche today is used to great advantage in plaited articles, butter-sticks, carnival-wähen, etc.

The direct fermentation process (Straight dough)

The direct system is well suited for most enriched yeast doughs where the ingredients are not extremely high and where the use of fruits is rather lower.

This takes in the doughs for larger Brioches, Streusel cakes, three king's cakes, Mozart plaits, Christmas Stollen, Neuenburger Taillaules, etc.

An addition of Levit raises not only the flavour but also improves the stability of the dough.

The bulk fermentation time

In the interests of a healthy dough development and the almost parallel build-up of flavour all doughs should have a bulk fermentation period of 60 minutes. One exception here is that of the plait dough with which a quarter of an hour fermentation time is sufficient, so that the working off of the plait can be done before the strands become too soft to handle.

Working off

Great skill is needed to work off doughs containing a lot of fruits and nuts. Already when weighing off the dough pieces great care is needed, for a break down of the dough at this point will have a greater detrimental effect later on. Care must be taken too in moulding the pieces to see that a smooth skin is created over the top and retained, without the fruit breaking out.

Baking off

In general, rich yeast doughs require to be baked in a cooler oven and mostly without steam and with an open damper. There are many reasons for this.

— Sugar rich doughs take colour more readily.
— Dough with a higher butter content will generally have liquid butter between the bottom of the articles and the sheet during the baking process. Even though this may only be a small amount it will quickly become over-heated and lead to burning of the bottom of the goods.

The picture shows, from left to right a perfectly moulded piece of well-worked dough. Next is shown the result of a strongly forced moulded piece from a similar well-worked dough. The fruits have cut through the skin of the dough with their sharp corners and will burn during the baking process. The dough piece on the right is from a dough which has not been mixed sufficiently, so that even though it has been carefully moulded it cannot achieve a smooth skin and can hardly hold the fruit in place.

— Many yeast dough goods are dusted with icing sugar, or spread over with macaroon-type mixtures before they are baked. If the temperature is too high at the start these may be flashed and burned. Similar problems may arise with nuts and kernels which are sprinkled on top of the goods.
— Too quick a baking of certain articles such as Panettoni, large Brioches and other goods can result in collapse and marking of the goods.

In order to avoid a creation of water from condensation on the bottoms of the goods, the yeast dough goods should be immediately placed on wires as soon as they are baked off.

The effect of the ingredients on the yeast dough

Ingredients used in yeast goods such as milk, butter and fats, eggs, sugar and dried fruits improve the quality of the articles as long as they are added to the optimum quantity. Apart from this they influence the condition of the dough, its fermentation capability and its baking properties.
Their effect is shown comprehensively in the following table:

Ingredients	Dough preparation	Fermentation process	Baking process	Characteristics
1. Fresh milk	Fine structure — fat part, fat distribution Tougher character — gluten strengthened by mineral salts — dough kneaded out well	Slightly retarded — mineral salt effect on the yeast — yeast quantity to be raised	Slightly less oven spring Stronger crust colour — milk sugar portion — much warmer oven	Soft crust Lively colour Fine, even light crumb Exceptional aroma and taste Longer freshness and keeping quality
2. Butter and fats	Very fine structure Plastic texture	Restrained with increased additions — inhibits yeast activity — increase yeast quantity	Less oven spring More intensive crust colour	Lively colour Short, delicate crust Fine crumb structure Even, light crumb Full aroma Good keeping quality
3. Eggs	Fine structure — emulsifying effect	Slightly retarded with increased quantities — inhibits yeast activity — increase yeast quantity Good proof tolerance — emulsifying effect, gas retention possibility	More intensive crust colour	Lively colour Delicate crust creation Strong crumb colour Finer pores Typical flavour note
4. Sugar	Hardly any effect	Retarded when over 200 g per kilo flour — yeast activity inhibited. Improved up to 200 g — acts as yeast food	Quicker browning reaction	Intensive colour Moister crumb Rounding off of flavour
5. Dried fruits	Less long dough structure — dough development inhibited — later addition	Start of fermentation speeded up — fruit sugar as a yeast food	Unfavourable around the edges — quicker hardening — strong browning	Characteristic baking properties Good retention of freshness

Königskuchen

(King's cake)

Publicity action by the Swiss Master bakers and confectioners Association

Large yeast goods, un-filled

Recipe

1 000 g milk
  150 g yeast
   50 g Levit
   10 g malt
  150 g sugar
   40 g salt
  100 g eggs
       lemon zest
  350 g butter
  150 g almond mixture
2 200 g to
2 000 g white flour
  300 g sultanas

Method

Break down the yeast, Levit, malt and sugar in the cold milk and knead to a finely worked dough with the flour. Mix the salt and lemon zest into the eggs, add at this stage and follow this with the butter, and the almond mixture. Knead further until the dough can be stretched and is fully plastic. Finally carefully mix through the sultanas which have been soaked in water and then drained off. Bulk fermentation time 60 to 90 minutes knock back once during this time.

Working off

Tightly mould up the centrepiece and the ring parts and place loosely together on greased sheets. Place a King's figure to each cake in one of the ring pieces which is placed around the outside of the middle piece. After full proof brush with egg. Sprinkle the centrepiece with white flake almonds, and the outside pieces too if desired. Bake in a not-too-hot oven. The selling factor of the article will be increased greatly by decorating the Königskuchen with a crown.

Size of the ring parts

Six-part cakes

Dough centrepiece	90 g
Dough ring parts to 40 g	240 g
Total weight	330 g

Eight-part cakes

Dough centrepiece	160 g
Dough ring parts to 40 g	320 g
Total weight	480 g

Ten-part cakes

Dough centrepiece	230 g
Dough ring parts to 40 g	400 g
Total weight	630 g

1st. August-Weggen

Publicity action by the Swiss Master bakers and confectioners Association

Recipe

1 000 g milk
100 g yeast
30 g Levit
20 g malt
50 g salt
100 g eggs
250 g butter
1 900 g white flour

Method

Work the ingredients to a well kneaded dough. Keep the dough as cool as possible. Bulk fermentation 60 minutes.

Working off

Mould dough pieces of 90 g or 240 g and place on sheets. Put the pieces to prove, then brush with egg and allow to stand in a cool place. Before baking cut with scissors as shown in the line sketch, to create a cross shape. Bake the 1st. August-Weggen in a medium hot oven to a golden yellow.

Guide to cutting the Swiss Cross (with scissors):

Neuenburger Taillaule

Dough

1 000 g milk
150 g yeast
20 g malt
400 g sugar
40 g salt
300 g eggs
lemon zest
300 g butter
2 300 g white flour
300 g orange-lemon peel
50 g rum

Method

Work the ingredients to a well-kneaded dough. Stir the eggs and salt together and add.

After two thirds of the kneading, add the butter. Finally add the orange-lemon peel, which has been soaked in the rum, carefully. Ferment the dough in a cool place for 60 to 90 minutes.

Working off

Weigh off the pieces and hand them up round first and then mould out to half the length of the cake tins being used. Place in the greased tins. After medium proof allow to stand out a little. Before baking brush with egg and cut with the scissors (Taillaule cut). Bake off in a medium oven without steam.

135

Gugelhopf

Ferment

500 g water
  50 g sour dough set
700 g white flour

Fermentation time 8 hours in a cold place.

Dough

1 200 g ferment
  500 g milk
  150 g yeast
   20 g malt
  400 g sugar
   30 g salt
  300 g egg yolk
1 500 g white flour
       lemon zest
  500 g butter
  750 g sultanas*
  100 g rum

*To increase the flavour, soak the sultanas in the rum overnight.

Method

Break down the yeast, malt and sugar in the milk. Add the ferment with the other ingredients with the exception of the egg yolk, salt, butter and sultanas and knead to a well worked dough. Stir the salt into the yolks and add in succession. Then add the butter and when this has been finely and smoothly worked in, carefully mix the fruit through the dough.
Bulk fermentation time approx. 90 minutes

Macaroon stollen

Working off

Mould up the weighed off pieces. Using a rolling pin create a hole in the middle and place the rings into the tins which have been greased with butter, with the closure uppermost. After a full proof, lightly brush with water or spray with water and bake in a fairly hot oven with steam. After baking, tip out onto a wire, allow to cool and then lightly dust with icing sugar.

Dough

1 000 g milk
  150 g yeast
   40 g Levit
   20 g malt
  300 g sugar
   50 g salt
  400 g eggs
       lemon zest
  300 g ground blanched almonds
2 400 g white flour
  300 g butter

Dresden stollen

Method

Mix all ingredients, with the exception of the butter to a well kneaded dough. Add the butter towards the end and leave in a cool place to ferment for approx. one hour.

Macaroon glaze

200 g fresh egg white
120 g sugar
200 g ground blanched
  almonds

Mix well together, but do not whisk to a foam.

Working off

Weigh off pieces of a size to suit the tins, hand up round and after a short recovery time mould long and place in the greased tins. After three-quarter proof spread with the macaroon mixture and cut a diamond pattern into the top surface with a sharp blade. Then dust with icing sugar and bake in a mild oven without steam to a golden yellow colour.

Sponge dough

1 000 g milk
  250 g yeast
1 800 g white flour

Fermentation time approx. 30 minutes.

Dough

3 000 g sponge dough
  500 g milk
   30 g salt
  500 g sugar
   40 g stollen spice mixture
1 750 g butter
2 500 g white flour
3 500 g sultanas
  500 g orange-lemon peel
  500 g blanched, chopped
    almonds
  150 g rum

Spice mixture

200 g vanilla sugar
 50 g ground nutmeg
150 g cardamom, ground
 50 g pepper

Mix all well together.

Method

Wash the fruit the day before and mix with the rum. Mix the sponge with the other ingredients but only using $1/3$ of the butter quantity and no fruit and knead to a dough. Then add a further $1/3$ of the butter and when the dough is smooth mix in the rest. After a further good kneading carefully mix the fruit through. Bulk fermentation time 20 to 30 minutes.

Working off

Mould the weighed off pieces to a long, almost rectangular piece. Place these on cloths with the closure uppermost. After a short resting time press firmly twice along the length, fold over and place on sheets lined with silicon paper. After a moderate proof bake in a medium hot oven. Brush the Stollen with butter while they are still hot. When fully cold roll in fine sugar crystals, and the next day dust over with icing sugar.

Panettone with sour dough ferment

1. Dough

950 g sour dough set
    (fully sour)
1 200 g water
  475 g butter
  560 g sugar
  440 g egg yolk
2 500 g white flour

Intensively work the water, sugar and flour with the ripe sour dough. Add the egg and butter a little at a time. Allow the dough to stand for 7 to 8 hours at 25 to 30°C. In this time the dough should have doubled its volume.

2. Dough

6 100 g 1. Dough
1 000 g water
  475 g butter
  560 g sugar
   50 g salt
  500 g egg yolk
1 400 g white flour
  625 g lemon or orange peel
3 100 g sultanas
    Fiori di Sicilia
    vanilla
    orange zest

Make up the second dough in a similar manner to the first. Knead until it is silky smooth. Then add the fruit.
Bulk fermentation 30 to 40 minutes.
Final proof 4 to 5 hours.

Panettone with yeast

Sponge dough

(Fermentation time approx. 8 hours)

500 g water
 20 g yeast
800 g white flour

Dough

1 300 g sponge dough
  500 g water
   70 g yeast
   40 g salt
  500 g sugar
   20 g malt
     Fiori di Sicilia
     lemon zest
  500 g butter
2 000 g white flour
  600 g egg yolk
  800 g sultanas
  400 g lime or orange peel,
     chopped

Method

Work the ferment well together and allow to prove at 30 to 35°C. Dissolve the sugar and malt in the water and mix with the ripe ferment. Knead to a dough with the flour. Stir the salt, lemon, Fiori di Sicilia and eggs together and add this a little at a time to the dough. Add the butter only when the dough is well developed. Knead the dough until it is fully developed and can be pulled out thinly. Carefully fold in the fruit right at the end.

Working off

Weigh off the dough pieces and mould up carefully. Remould twice over a period of approx. 30 minutes and then place in the special Panettone paper moulds. Proof of the finished pieces 3 to 4 hours. Cut the fully proved Panettone slightly with a sharp knife over into a cross and put a piece of butter in the centre.

Place in a good hot oven and take out again as soon as a skin has formed; approx. 2 minutes. Carefully open the skin on the cuts again and lay the skin back in its original place.

Immediately bake off in a medium hot oven and steam well. When the Panettone are fully developed open the damper and bake out to a light colour.

139

Colomba di Pasqua

(Easter Dove)

Sponge dough

1 000 g water
100 g sour dough set
250 g sugar
200 g egg yolk
1 700 g white flour, approx.

Ferment 7 to 8 hours.

Dough

3 200 g Sponge dough
1 000 g water
100 g yeast
250 g sugar
40 g malt
200 g egg yolk
50 g salt
650 g butter
600 g candied fruits
400 g coarse almonds
3 000 g white flour
vanilla
Fiori di Sicilia

Dough with yeast

Ferment

1 000 g water
100 g Levit
100 g yeast
1 000 g white flour

Fermentation approx. 3 hours.

Dough

2 400 g sponge dough
1 000 g milk
100 g yeast
400 g sugar
40 g malt
400 g egg yolk
50 g salt
600 g butter
600 g candied fruits
400 g coarse almonds
3 000 g white flour
vanilla
Fiori di Sicilia

Spreading mass

350 g egg whites
140 g sugar
280 g finely ground hazelnuts

well mixed together

Method

Mix the ingredients in the usual manner to a finely kneaded dough. Add the egg yolk a little at a time and the butter later. Carefully fold in the fruits at the end of the kneading process.
Bulk fermentation time 90 to 120 minutes.

Working off

It is recommended that tins are used. Take two pieces of dough of the size to suit the tins, mould them round and then long. Halve one of the pieces and shape it to an oval. Place the larger piece in length into the tin to create the body and the two smaller pieces on the left and right sides to represent the wings. After a short resting time spread the top surface with the spreading mass. Press 10 whole almonds in the top, use a half red cherry for the eye and sprinkle with nib sugar. Finally dust well with icing sugar and bake out in a medium hot oven without steam to a light colour.

Mozart plait

Dough

1 000 g milk
150 g yeast
30 g Levit
10 g malt
200 g sugar
30 g salt
200 g eggs
300 g butter
2 200 g white flour
150 g finely chopped orange-
lemon peel

Method

Break down the yeast, Levit, malt and sugar in the milk and mix the flour. Stir the salt in the egg and add to the dough. Add the butter first when the dough is finely worked and finally work in the fruits. Work the dough off immediately.

Working off

Roll out 8 equal size dough pieces (80 to 150 g) to spindle shaped strands and plait (see page 177). With a medium proof allow to stand in a cooler place. Before baking brush with egg and bake out in a medium hot oven with an open damper. While still hot, apricot, glaze and sprinkle with a few flake almonds.

Bündner-pitta

Sponge dough

1 000 g water
150 g yeast
100 g Levit
1 800 g white flour

Mixture

3 000 g sponge dough
400 g butter
200 g sugar
200 g almond mixture 1:1
250 g eggs
40 g salt
lemon zest
vanilla
1 000 g sultanas

Method

Break down the yeast and Levit in the water, mix to a dough with the flour and allow to ferment for approx. 40 minutes. In between cream the other ingredients, except for the sultanas, and then add this mass to the dough a little at a time. Gently fold the sultanas in at the end.
Bulk fermentation approx. 60 minutes.

Working off

Weigh 300 g dough pieces and mould round, pin out and place in tins or rings of 18 cm diameter. Press out to the edge, allow to prove well, brush with egg and dock well. Sprinkle 20 g split almonds and 30 g nib sugar on each, dust with icing sugar and bake to a light colour in a medium oven without steam.

Sweet yeast dough plaits

Sweet yeast dough

1 000 g milk
  150 g yeast
   50 g Levit
   20 g malt
  200 g sugar
   40 g salt
  100 g eggs
  200 g butter
2 000 g white flour
      lemon zest
      vanilla

Method

Break down the yeast, Levit, malt and sugar in the milk, and well knead with the flour to a dough. Mix the salt, eggs and flavours and add to the dough a little at a time. Finally add the butter and work off the finished dough immediately.

Working off

Roll out 200 g dough pieces to spindle shaped strands. Plait three or four of these strands to a spindle shaped plait (see pages 166 to 169) and place on sheets. After a medium proof, remove to a cool place, brush with egg and bake in a moderate oven with the damper open. While hot, apricot each piece, thinly glaze and sprinkle on each a little flake almond or nib sugar.

Fillings

Streusel cakes

Large yeast goods, filled

Brown filling I

1 000 g almonds or hazelnuts, finely ground
800 g sugar
200 g glucose
10 g cinnamon
500 g water

Finely mill the ingredients with half of the water. Eventually thin with water to the desired consistency.

White filling 1:1

1 000 g white almonds
1 000 g sugar
400 g water

Mill the ingredients finely together and then thin to the desired consistency with egg white or water. Use lemon zest and Kirsch for flavour.

Dough

1 000 g milk
150 g yeast
50 g Levit
20 g malt
150 g sugar
40 g salt
200 g eggs
cinnamon
lemon zest
250 g butter
2 100 g white flour

Method

Knead the ingredients together to a dough in the usual manner. Allow to ferment in a cool place for approx. 60 minutes.

Streusel

1. Butter-streusel

300 g white flour
300 g sugar
250 g butter

2. Hazelnut-streusel

150 g white flour
150 g finely ground hazelnuts
300 g sugar
225 g butter

Brown filling II

1 000 g almonds or hazelnuts, finely ground
300 g sponge crumbs
5 g cinnamon
2 g lemon zests
600 g sugar
600 g water, approx.

Boil the sugar and water and mix with the other ingredients. Fillings made by this method will remain moist longer.

Bienenstich

(Bee stings)

Method for the streusel

First ensure that the butter is worked creamy and then mix with the other ingredients and rub together to form a compact mass. Do not work too much or the mass will become greasy. Allow to set for a time in the fridge and then pass through a coarse sieve with mesh of about 5 mm.

Working off

Mould up the dough pieces round and then pin out. Fill into the appropriate rings and dock well. After a medium proof allow to stand in a cool place for a short time, brush with egg and sprinkle with the streusel. Bake in a moderate oven without steam. When cold, split and fill with Diplomat creme (e.g. vanilla creme / whipped cream 2:1). Dust with icing sugar.

Dough

As for Streusel cakes.

Topping

200 g butter
150 g honey
100 g sugar
 50 g glucose
     lemon zest

boil all together

300 g white, flake almonds

Stir the almonds into the boiling mixture.

Working off

Mould dough pieces round and then pin out. Fill into the rings and dock well. After a fair proof stand in a cool place for a while. Then spread the mixture, cooled, not too thick but as evenly as possible, all over the top. Bake in a moderate oven without steam. Cut when cold and fill with the Diplomat creme (e.g. vanilla creme / whipped cream 2:1 flavoured with Kirsch).

Party nut horns

Dough

1 000 g milk
  150 g yeast
   50 g Levit
   20 g malt
  200 g sugar
   40 g salt
  100 g eggs
  200 g butter
2 000 g white flour
      lemon zest
      vanilla

Method

Break down the yeast, Levit, malt and sugar in the milk and knead to a dough with the flour. Stir the salt into the egg and add. Finally add the butter and knead the dough very well. Bulk fermentation time approx. 1½ hours.

Working off

Weigh off dough pieces at 300 g and mould. After a short recovery period pin out to large triangles. Spread 200 g hazelnut or almond filling per horn. Then roll up and place on sheets.
Brush with egg before baking and possibly lightly dock. Bake in a moderate oven with steam. Apricot the Party horns while still hot, glaze and sprinkle with flake almonds.

Carré-stollen

(Diamond stollen)

Dough

1 000 g milk
  200 g yeast
   50 g Levit
   20 g malt
  400 g sugar
   50 g salt
  200 g eggs
  600 g butter
  400 g fine, white almonds
2 400 g white flour
      lemon zest

Method

Work the ingredients to a dough in the normal way. Stir the egg and salt together and add. Knead the dough well. Add the butter half way through the mixing time and the ground almonds right at the end.
Bulk fermentation time 60 to 90 minutes.

Filling

1 500 g hazelnuts or almonds
  600 g orange peel
1 200 g sugar
  600 g water

Mill finely and thin down with water to a spreading consistency.

Working off

Pin out dough pieces to 25 × 30 cm, spread with the filling, and fold the piece over twice on the long side. Place on sheets or in tins.
After a full proof brush twice with egg, cut with a blade to produce the diamond pattern and bake to a light colour in a mild oven.

Birnenweggen

(Pear rolls)

Dough
(laminated)

1 000 g white flour
  400 g butter
   25 g salt
   30 g yeast
   10 g malt
   50 g sugar
  350 g water

Method

Rub together the flour, butter and salt. Mix to a dough with the other ingredients. Give 3 single turns and allow to ferment in a cool place for 40 to 50 minutes.

Filling
(pear mass)

1 000 g poached pear pieces
       (Dried.)
  400 g figs
  200 g poached dried prunes
       (damsons)
  100 g apple or apricot jam
  100 g sugar
   50 g pear-bread spice
  100 g pear brandy
  200 g sultanas or currants

(possibly some chopped walnuts sprinkled over the spread filling).

Method

Boil the pears and prunes together and pass through a hand mincer with the figs. Then add the rest of the ingredients. Thin to a spreading consistency with pear water (water in which the pears have been boiled).

Pear-bread spice

100 g ground aniseed
100 g cinnamon
 50 g cloves
 50 g nutmeg
 50 g coriander

Working off the Birnenweggen

Pin out the dough 2 mm thick and cut out to the desired sizes. Spread the filling over the surface in the proportion of 1 : 1 or even pipe it on top. Possibly sprinkle with chopped walnuts. Place both long sides over the middle and place on sheets with the closure underneath. Brush immediately with egg and leave to prove. Before baking, brush again with egg, mark with a fork, dock and bake out in a moderate oven with the damper open, to a pale colour.

Bündner Birnenbrot

(Pear bread)

Bündner Birnenbrot is distinguished from other types in that the dried and cut pears are not boiled, but rather are soaked for 12 to 18 hours in rosewater and pear brandy.

Pear mass

3 000 g dark bread dough, fully ripe
3 000 g dried cleaned pears ⎤ Cut to
750 g figs ⎥ small
250 g orange peel ⎥ slices
250 g lemon peel ⎥ with the
250 g cedrat peel ⎦ slicing machine
750 g sultanas
750 g pear brandy
750 g rosewater
750 g walnuts
40 g pear-bread spice

Pear-bread spice mixture

200 g cinnamon
100 g star-anised
150 g anised
10 g pepper

Method

Pour the pear-brandy over all of the mixed fruit, add the rosewater, mix well and leave covered for 12 to 18 hours. Then mix with the well ripened bread dough, and the spice until it gives a homogenous mass. Possibly add 2 to 3 dl water. Finally fold in the walnuts. Now allow the whole dough mixture to recover for 90 to 120 minutes.

Dough for enclosing

Recipe

1 000 g milk
80 g yeast
20 g malt
100 g sugar
40 g salt
100 g butter
1 600 g white flour

Well knead the ingredients to a dough in the usual manner. It is enough to enclose the following mass, in proportions of:

900 g pear mass
200 g enclosing dough or
450 g pear mass
100 g enclosing dough

Working off

Weigh off pieces of the pear dough at 450 or 900 g and shape these into rectangles of approx. 16 cm or 24 cm squares.
Place the pieces on well dusted boards and leave, covered, for 90 to 120 minutes. Enclose the pear dough in the enclosing dough as follows:
Weigh off the enclosing dough and first hand it up to long shapes. Then pin it out to rectangles, but not too large in size. Brush the surface with water and on top place the pear mass from which all of the flour has been removed. Fold the dough over from all sides and seal well together. Allow to prove for 10 to 15 minutes, then brush with egg. Mark with a fork and dock. According to size bake at approx. 240°C for 40 to 50 minutes, without steam. Do not open the door during the first 20 minutes, otherwise the dough may split open. Next day, enclose in shrink-wrap foil. In this way the bread will keep fresh for several weeks.

Glarner Birnenbrot

(Pear bread)

Pear mass

2000 g dark bread dough, well
      ripened
2000 g dried
      pears,
      cleaned, ⎫ coarsely
      boiled ⎬ chopped
  300 g orange-
      lemon peel
  300 g figs
  200 g walnuts
  600 g raisins
  600 g sugar
  200 g Kirsch, rum or
      red wine
    40 g ground anised
    40 g cinnamon
    20 g cloves
    20 g ground nutmeg

Method

Mix the bread dough with the
other ingredients to a medium
tight dough. Do not over-
knead so that the pears
remain whole. Allow the mass
to ferment for 90 to 120
minutes.

Dough for enclosing

500 g milk
  50 g yeast
  10 g malt
  50 g sugar
  20 g salt
  50 g butter
800 g white flour

Work the ingredients to a
dough in the normal manner,
kneading well. It serves to
enclose the previous mass in
proportions of:

900 g pear mass
200 g enclosing dough
      or
450 g pear mass
100 g enclosing dough

**Large yeast
articles from
laminated
sweet dough**

Laminated yeast dough

Pastry made from laminated yeast dough counts as one of the finest articles which the baker can produce. The essentials in the production of this dough are the exact enclosing as well as the turning, which is only slightly different from the process of puff pastry making.

The various types of dough

Basically one differentiates between three types of laminated yeast dough.

Dough type	Best known pastries
Crescent dough	Paris crescents, Caraway rolls
Sweet yeast dough	Mainly, filled, large, yeast dough pieces
Plunder dough	Small and large Plunder pastries (Danish pastries)

Dough production

For all three types of dough, the yeast, bread improver, malt and sugar are broken down in the very cold milk, the salt is stirred into the eggs and this is then kneaded in with the other ingredients and the flour. A stronger kneading is recommended with stronger flours.
Almost immediately after the kneading process, the dough is divided into pieces of the size required for the turning process. These are usually 1 to 1,5 liter, or 3,5 to 5 kg dough.
Eventually the dough pieces are shaped to rectangles and placed to rest in the cold.

Enclosing

In principle the consistency of the fat to be enclosed should correspond with that of the dough. Too firm fat will not roll out evenly. Too soft fat will squeeze out during turning, or else be taken into the layers and mix through them. Either one will give poor separation and so very uneven lifting of the pastry. The fat is evenly placed over 2/3 of the surface of the pinned out dough, then the uncovered third of the dough is folded over the middle third and finally the whole is folded over again.

Turning

The dough is now given 3 simple turns with regular resting periods between each turn. In this way one achieves an alternating of layers of dough and fat structure which serves to give a leafy, airy baked structure. Two aspects are of great importance in the turning: the rolling out of the dough thickness and the number of turns given. The end effect of both factors concerns the thickness of the layers and the aeration.
In order to minimise the tearing open or pressing out of the fat layers it is very important to pin out in gentle steps, that is to say, not to try to roll out to the ideal thickness of layers too quickly.

Thickness of turns

The pictures show the results of baking tests carried out on Crescent paste, which is based on a dough quantity of 1 liter of liquid which has been given 3 simple turns of 6 to 14mm.

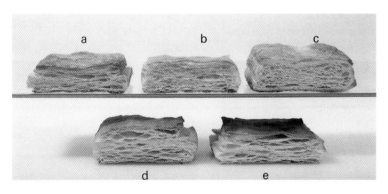

Baking test	Turned thickness mm	Result on the pastries
a	6	Too fine a layer. Loss of leafiness, soft
b	8	Good, but still under the border
c	10	Ideal, typical layers and leafiness
d	12	Rather coarser layers with light tendency for the fat to run out
e	14	Too coarse, fat runs out, a little hard and brittle

The number of turns has a similar effect to that of the thickness of the turns, on the leafiness of the pastry.

Number of turns

The pictures show the baking tests f to k of how the more-or-fewer turns, which were all of 10 mm, affected the pastries.

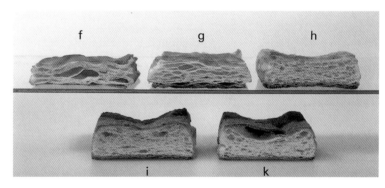

Baking test	Number of turns	Result on the pastries
f	1	Too thick a layer, strong running out, Weggli-dough appearance
g	2	Layers still too thick, light running out, very uneven structure
h	3	Ideal aeration and structure
i	4	Equally very good
k	5	Rather uneven, poor structure by comparison to h and i

Laminated sweet yeast dough

Russian plait

Dough

1 000 g	milk
150 g	yeast
30 g	Levit
20 g	malt
200 g	sugar
40 g	salt
100 g	eggs
	lemon zest
100 g	butter
2 000 g	white flour
600 g	butter to be enclosed

Method

Break down the yeast, Levit, malt and sugar in the cold milk and then mix with the flour. Stir the salt into the egg and lemon zest and add to the dough. Finally add the butter and knead well. Pin out the dough to a rectangle and divide the plasticised butter over ⅔ of its surface and enclose it. Give three simple turns at intervals of 10 to 15 minutes. It can then be worked off after a rest of 30 to 50 minutes or be left covered overnight in a very cool place (in this case only use 100 g of yeast per liter).

Working off

Pin out the dough piece to a rectangle and spread with brown almond or hazelnut filling. Roll up, and then cut in the middle down the length. Cross the two parts over each other with the cut surfaces uppermost and plait them together. Place on sheets or in rectangular tins. After a good proof bake the plaits in a fairly hot oven. While hot, brush with apricot and glaze. Sprinkle a little nib sugar or flake almond in the centre.

Yeast ring

Filled yeast circle

Working off

Pin out laminated yeast dough to a rectangle and spread with brown filling. Sprinkle with sultanas and roll up. Shape into a ring and place this in greased rings with the closure uppermost. Allow to prove and then bake in a moderate oven with steam. Turn out, apricot, glaze and enclose the edge with fine hazelnuts.

Working off

Pin out laminated yeast dough to a rectangle and cut into 3 equally wide strips down the length. Pipe almond filling on top with a plain tube. Roll these up and plait. Place the plaited pieces onto a sheet and form them into a ring. Place a round mould in the centre of the ring and around its outside. Allow to prove, brush with egg and bake. While still hot, apricot and glaze and sprinkle with lightly roast flake almonds.

Roll cakes

Sun

Working off

Pin out laminated yeast dough to a rectangle, spread with almond filling and roll up. From it cut pieces 2,5 to 3 cm wide, place these in a thin or in a mould on a sheet. After proving brush with egg and bake. While still hot, apricot and glaze. Sprinkle with flake white almonds.

Method

Pin out laminated sweet dough 3 mm thick and from it cut out rounds of 24 cm diameter. Spread 200 g white almond mixture, 1×1 on each, brush the top surface with egg and place a second circle of dough on top as a lid. Cut deeply into the edge around to 4 cm deep, twist these individual cuts (approx. 16) and turn them over. Brush the whole article with egg and

sprinkle the centre with flaked almonds. After a good proof brush the turned-back parts with egg and bake in a pre-steamed, mild oven. When baked, dust the centre part with icing sugar, apricot the outer part while it is still hot and glaze.

Tip: With large-scale production, the almond mixture can be placed between sheets of silicon paper and pinned out to approx. 6 mm.

Piccadilly

Week-end stollen

Production

Pin out laminated sweet dough to 3 mm thick and cut from it round pieces of 24 cm diameter. Spread 200 g almond mixture 1×1 onto each of these bases, brush he top surface with egg and place a second circle of dough on top as a lid. Using a 14 cm ring, make a mark in the centre. In this centre now cut four points in the shape of a star and brush the whole with egg. Take the points which were formed by the cuts and place them across the outside. Again brush with egg. Place a ring in the centre opening. After a good proof dock under the points with a pointed knife. Brush again with egg and bake to a light colour in a medium oven. While still hot, apricot and glaze and decorate with 8 candied cherries.

Production

Pin out 1 kg of laminated sweet dough to a rectangle of 25 × 72 cm. Spread 500 g white almond filling on the top surface, sprinkle some candied fruits over that and roll it up. Cut the roll into four even pieces of 18 cm and place it on a silicon lined sheet, or a greased baking sheet. Cut each piece 7 to 8 times with the scissors quite deeply, and pull this pieces to the centre and cross over alternately to each side. Prove the stollen, brush with egg and bake out in a fairly hot oven. Apricot and glaze immediately after baking.

Plaited breads

History

The well-loved plaited bread is not only known throughout Switzerland, but also throughout much of Europe. What is not so well known, is that the plait bread owes its origins to an ancient cult, that of the Ladies- or Hair sacrifices. In ancient times it was the custom that, with the death of the man of the family, the wife had to be buried with him so that they could both go to the other side together. So, as this barbaric custom slowly disappeared it left behind the hair sacrifice in place of the Lady sacrifice. The women cut off their long plaits and placed them with their lords and masters in the grave. This is proved by various examples from the Greek literature. So we can read in the "Iliad" that the slaves covered the bodies with their cut-off hair. In the work of Euripides "Iphigenie on Taurus" we read that Orestes awaited that his sister should cover his grave with her tears and hair.

For the comfort and health of an expected child the Greek women sacrificed their hair to the Goddness of health "Hygieia". The hair sacrifice was also known to the old Germanen. Later however, cutting off the hair was a sign of bondage and knavery.

A survival of the hair sacrifice is today seen in the tonsure of the Monks and the cutting-off of the hair before the dressing of a Nun. As the hair sacrifice took the place of the human sacrifice, so that cult also was substituted, in that later in place of the plait of hair, its representation in bread was used. With the influence of Christianity in the middle ages, in place of putting the bread in the graves, it was shared out among the poor of the region. In this manner we have today in many places the "Seelenbrotes" (bread of the soul) or "Seelenzöpfe" (soul plait) which are given to the God-children and poor people on All Souls Day and at New Years Eve. As time went on, other bread such as rings and rolls came to be used too as "Soul bread".

With the development of the baking trade this representative bread was also refined. In place of bread dough a richer dough came to be used made of white flour with additives of butter, and for special tastes also eggs, sugar and sultanas were added. Earlier, the plaits were made for very special festive dates, such as Christmas and New Year. Today one finds plaits almost daily in the bakery trade.

Production and fermentation

In order to achieve a faultless, finely presented plait, the creation of the recipe and the care of the fermentation is of outstanding importance. The best results are achieved with a short and cool fermentation period. The longer a dough lies, the more difficult it will be to work off, and the less will be the volume. The cooler the dough the less will be the possibility of it skinning as it is worked off. This again will influence the proof for the better. In order to give a better flavour to the plait, it is recommended that it be made with a sponge and dough process, or with an additive such as Levit. The use of overnight, direct fermentation has not found favour in connection with the appearance of the plait, and the flavour.

The ingredients

These not only have a qualitative influence on the plaits, but also on their appearance. The ingredients in the following recipes are carefully balanced out., i.e. more butter and eggs do not give any improvement. An egg additive gives a softer crumb structure and refines the crust. This will be smoother and have a much more satin gloss. The assumption that the plait will be drier is not true, but with the finer structure and the larger volume, it will dry out more quickly. An addition of 20 to 30 g sugar per liter will keep the plait fresh for a longer time.

The production and handling of the dough

It is important to create the dough first, without the addition of egg or butter. These ingredients should only be added after the dough has actually been created in order to make as short and smooth a dough as possible. Plait doughs are very good to handle. The kneading time can vary according to the type of machine to be used. A normal dough mixer will take 15 to 20 mintues, a fast mixer not longer than 10 to 15 minutes.

Working off the plaits

A good, even working of the strands is of the greatest importance to the shape and appearance of the plait. With plaiting care must be taken that the individual strands are all equally tightly and evenly moulded as possible in plaiting. In this way the plait will get an even break. Before baking, brush twice with egg with a short pause between each. To get the important break, the correct individual proof is vital. It should be kept rather on the shorter side. During this time the plait should be covered with a plastic sheet. Leaving the pieces out for a short time before baking will also help with the breaking evenly.

Baking

The correct temperature of the oven has a lot to do with a good appearance. If the oven is too cool then the loaf will run out flatter with a strong rip in the top surface. Too hot an oven will cause it to break at the sides while it will remain blind on top. Plaited loaves need to be baked off at approx. 20 to 30°C below the baking temperature for bread, and if possible always on the oven bottom. The dough acids which form during the fermentation, create an oxidation on a baking sheet, which can carry marks over to the plait during baking, and can give it an unappetising flavour. This is not quite so much the case with aluminium or chrome-steel baking sheets. If it is not possible to avoid baking on a normal baking sheet, then the plait should be removed onto boards as soon as they are baked off, and left there to cool.

Recipe

Butter zopf

1 000 g milk (approx. 20°C)
    50 g Levit
  100 g yeast
    40 g salt
    20 g malt
  100 g eggs
  300 g butter
1 800 g white flour

Whole wheat butter zopf

1 000 g water
    60 g yeast
    50 g Levit
    10 g malt
    30 g salt
    50 g eggs
  500 g butter
1 700 g whole wheat flour
      extra fine

Plait of two strands, plaited flat

This plait is commonly known as a Farmer's plait. The system of plaiting creates a fine picture. The centre part becomes quite prominent and shows itself in a diamond pattern.

Place two evenly rolled-out dough strands over each other crossways. Place the underneath strand over the upper strand first, and cross it over itself. Then place the right part of the second strand over the right end of the first. The left side now consists of three strands. The outer strand left is now placed under the one next to it and then placed over the next strand on the right strand. The outermost right strand again over the next one on the left side, so that three strands again are formed on the left side. Carry on as described in plaiting the outermost left, and repeat the steps described from left and right.

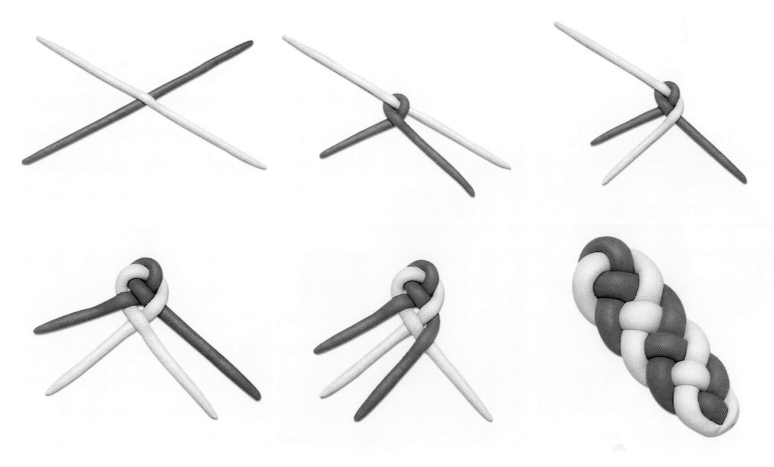

Plait of two strands, plaited high

This is the most used plait. Its method of plaiting is the same everywhere. Its shape however is often different. In the Canton of Berne the plait is broad and blunt. In Central Swiss it is made broad and flat. The East Swiss people however like a longer, thinly woven plait.

Place two evenly rolled out strands across each other. One gets hold of the two ends of the bottom strand and pulls them over the second strand in that the strand ends lie over the left side of the right end and over the second strand. With the second strand one moves it with the right part over the left part of the first strand, and with the left part also over the right part of the first, as over its own strand. Then follows the move with the first, and then the second strand, until the plait is plaited to its end.

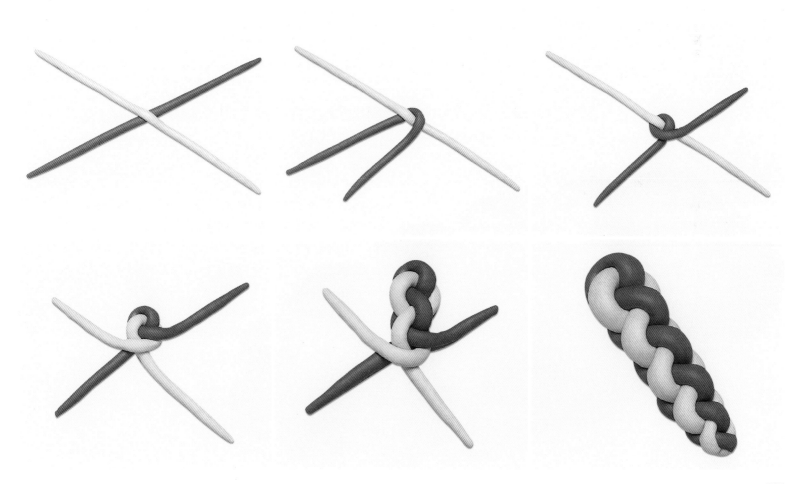

Three-pieces plait, plaited flat

Here we are dealing with the original plaiting process. It has carried over to today as the plait for hair pigtails.

This type of plaiting is very easy. But it still provides plenty of variety to your assortment.

To commence the plaiting, take two strands to the right and one strand to the left, on the table. Pass the outer right hand strand inside of the left hand strand so that it becomes the left inner strand. Now take the left outer strand over to the inside right. Carry on alternately in this manner with the right or the left strand until the plait is woven to its end.

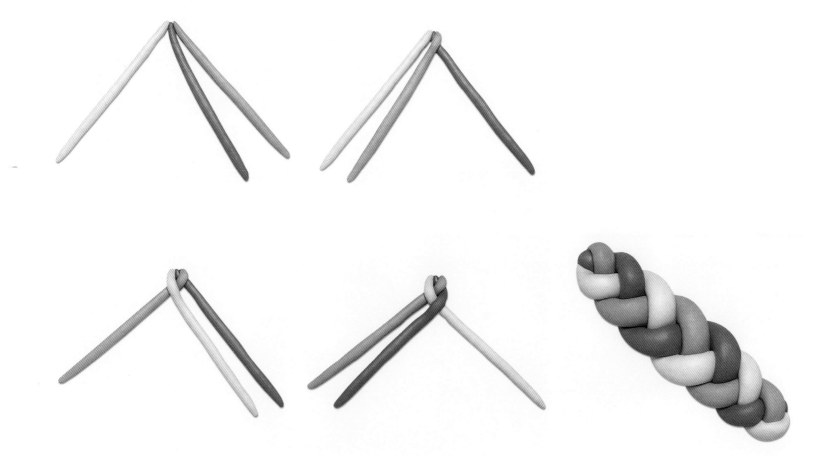

Four-piece plait, plaited flat, spindle shaped

This plait is often made in country districts. It can be used easily for plaited loaves such as Golatsch etc.

Commence with two strands to the left and two strands to the right. One carries on with taking the outer strands left and right and placing them over the strand next to each. The strand is placed on the inside of the left pair of strands. Pull the strand on the extreme left under the one next to it and over the following one, to lie on the inside of the right strand. Now carry the outer right over the one next to it once again. Then follows the move with the left strand in which it is passed under the next one to it, and over the following one. These phases are now repeated until the end.

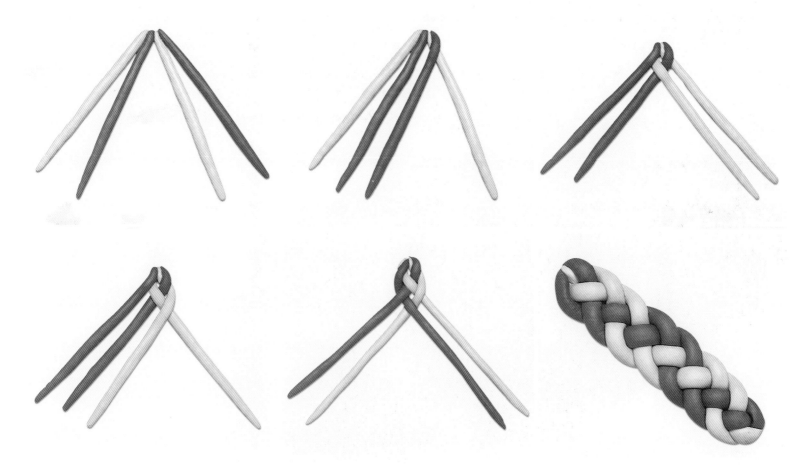

Five-piece plait, plaited flat

This method of plaiting can be used with strands of greater number, as long as they are always uneven. The more strands that are used, the broader the plaited bread will be. So this fact itself will set the limit on the number of strands used.

The plaiting follows a similar pattern to that of the three-plait, flat. One side must always have an uneven number of strands. The outside strand is then taken and placed by the side of the opposite strand. So the opposite side now has the odd number of strands. So, using this outside strand, it can continuously be woven with the outside strand backwards and forwards.

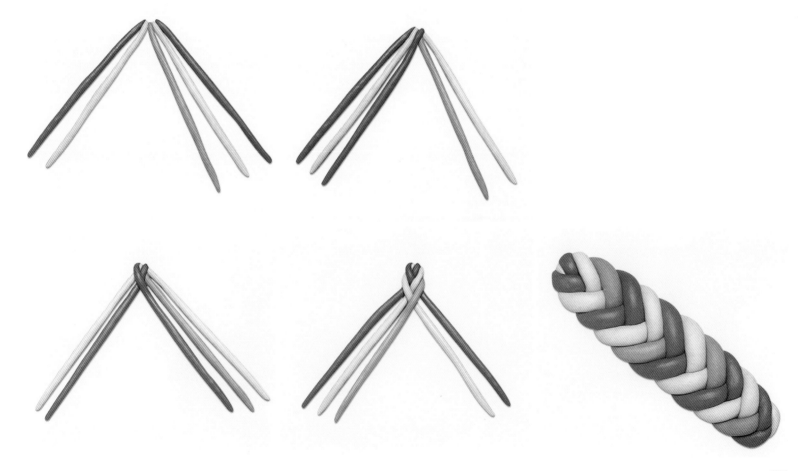

Five-piece plait, plaited high

The five-piece plait is not only a well presented article in its own right, it is often used in the presentation of show-pieces. For it, one needs five strands of equal size, but each a little thicker in the middle. The plaiting pattern is not too difficult and consists of two constantly repeated moves. The finished plait is spindle shaped and must be turned over onto one side, so that one prominent strand lies on top and follows the path of the spindle shaping. It is started with the two outside strands. The strand on the extreme right is pulled through under the left strand and put in its place. The left strand is now placed in the middle. Now the strand which has been put in the middle is changed with the strand next to it on the left, in that it is passed underneath. These two moves are constantly repeated as described, in that the two outer strands are crossed, the left strand placed in the middle, and then its place changed with the one next to it. For show-pieces it is often necessary (particularly with the butterfly and heart) to mould one piece from left to right and another from right to left, so that the spirals run from left to right in one piece and from right to left in the other. To do this one commences with the three strands on the left. The method from then is the same, only that one goes from left and not from right.

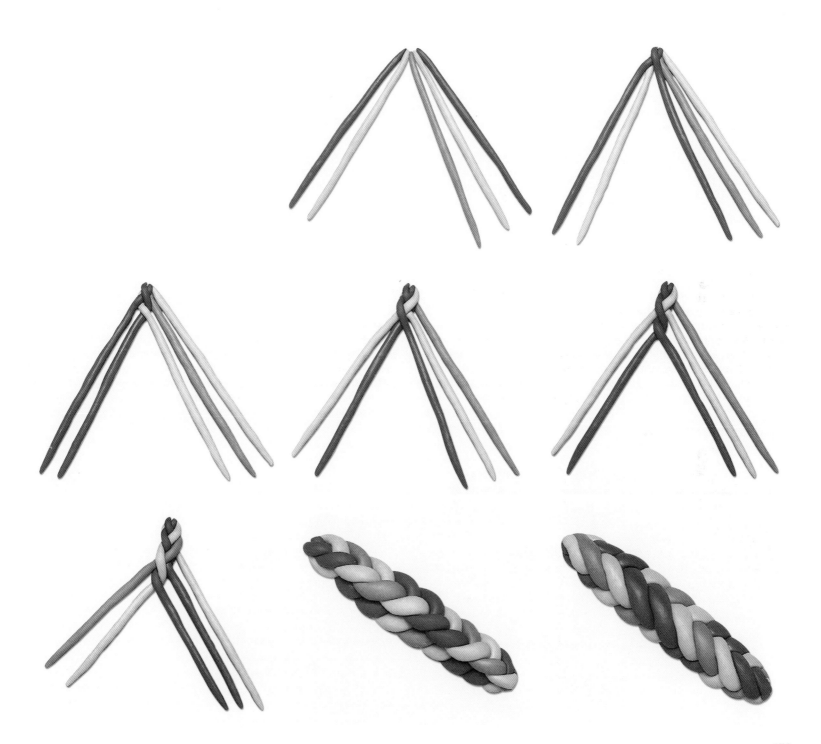

Six-piece plait

The plait made up from six strands is very attractive. It is also called Wiener Stritzel, that is the plaiting pattern of Stritzel. To make it one needs six even sized, spindle shaped pieces of dough. To get the best plait shape it is recommended to keep the strands a little thicker in the middle. The pattern of plaiting is a little more difficult as it must always be plaited counter-hand. The main characteristic for this pattern is the creation of the so-called little windows on both sides of the plait. In order to keep these perfectly even, a tight regular plaiting is of great importance. The six dough strands are always kept in two groups of three during the whole of the process. At the start the outer strands of both goups are crossed over. From this, the left group consists all the time of 1 strand upper right and two strands lower left. The right group in contrast has 1 strand upper left and two strands lower right. The further moves are then always to be followed inside one of the groups. One starts with the left group, in that the right strand is raised and the left exterior strand is changed under it. This raised strand thus is now put in, to be the left inside strand. Now follows the move on the right side. The upper strand on the left is raised and the right outside strand is put under in its place. Again the raised strand is put down to become the right inner strand. The plait is now to be plaited out to its end with the two groups being plaited in this manner, one after the other.

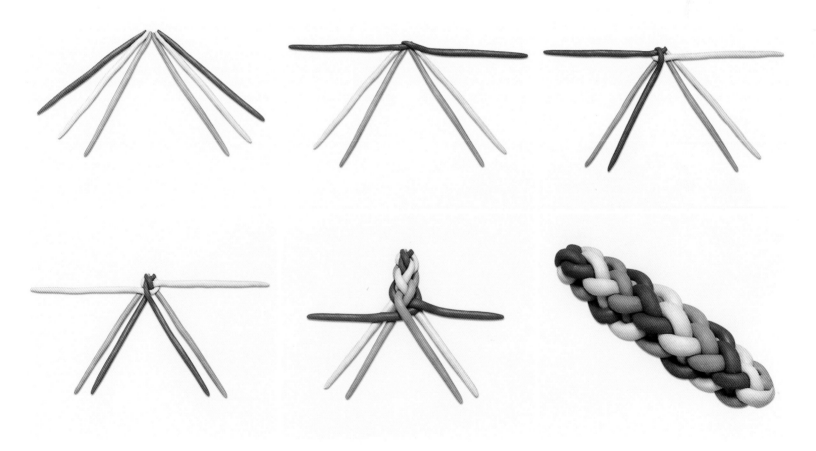

Eight-piece plait

One needs eight even sized dough strands, slightly thicker in the middle, to create this plait. When made with a sweet yeast plait dough, it is known mainly as a Mozart plait. The plaiting as such is not difficult as the moves are repeated constantly. The eight strands are divided into two groups of four on the table, with the ends of all eight being tightly fastened together. As with the six-part plait, except for the first move, the plaiting is done within two groups. First cross the two outer strands of the two groups with each other and place over the top of the other strands. The right group now consists of three strands below right and one strand left above. The left group has the three strands under left, and one strand above right. The plaiting starts with the left group in that the strand right above is put down as the left inner strand, while the left exterior strand right above is put in its place. Now one commences on the right group, where the upper left strand is changed with the right inner strand, while the right exterior strand is changed to the left upper strand. These plaiting moves are now carried on alternately with the left and right groups to the end to the plait as a whole.

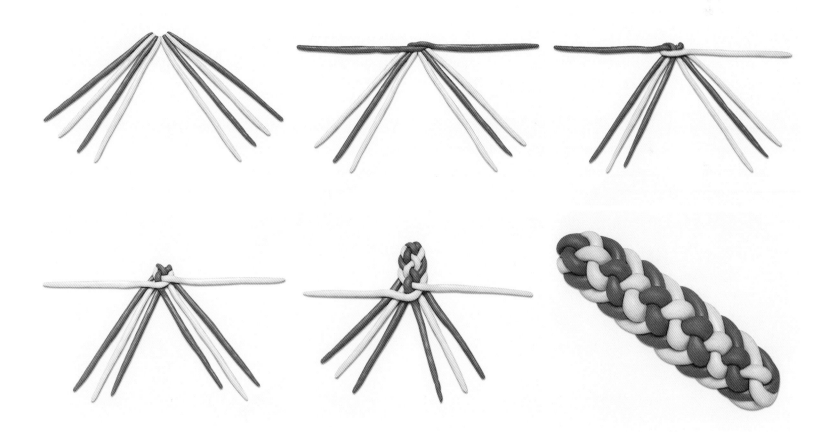

Zopf bread

Direct fermentation

```
1 000 g  milk, approx. 15°C
   35 g  salt
   20 g  malt
  100 g  yeast
   50 g  Levit
  400 g  eggs
  300 g  sugar
  300 g  butter
3 000 g  white flour, approx.
    1    lemon
```

Method

Make up a dough in the usual manner and allow to ferment for approx. one hour.

Working off

Weigh off six equal pieces of dough for each loaf; these being plaited together in two sets of three. Plait them together as for a plait of two strands in the flat. The weave must be kept short. Turn the whole over with the closure below and make into a round. The bread is to be so arranged that one of the three-plaits is in the middle. After a proof, brush the dough with egg. Cut the tips on the top with scissors and bake in a moderate oven

Plaited bread articles

Clover-leaf

With imagination and a little skill it is fairly simple to create baked articles for special occasions, and festivals. Plaited pieces serve excellently for this work. However, the following points should be observed:
1. Keep the dough a little tight, but select a short and strong fermentation process.
2. Keep the parts of the figure always in proportion.
3. Keep the plaited parts quite thin, otherwise the articles will be too plump.
4. Before baking, brush the articles two or three times with egg.
5. Such plaited articles are usually kept to a large size. So the oven should not be too hot, so that the articles will bake out sufficiently and at the same time get a fine, golden yellow colour.

One needs three five-part plaits for its production. One should ensure that they are kept rather long and thinly plaited. A twisted strand serves as the stalk. Join all of the ends together in the middle and cover with a rosette. This show-piece can also be made with four leaves and can be used for many festive dates, such as New Year, Jubilees, Christening, Birthday etc.

Butterfly

This is created with four, five-part plaits. Two of these must have been plaited from left to right. That is to say that at the start of the plaiting there must be three strands to the left and two to the right. The other two plaits are to be plaited in the normal manner; that is to say that they must start with three strands on the right. One will also need three pieces of dough for the head, front body and rear part of the body, as well as two small pieces for the feelers. The wings can also be filled in with thin dough strings. Care should be taken that the body parts are not too thick, but kept quite graceful in appearance. Mark with a knife before baking.

Lyre

This is made from one large five-part plait. The plait should not be too thick, so that it can be shaped nicely. Four thinner dough strands, held together with a small, three-part plait to represent the strings.

Star, plaited high

From the illustration of the work being carried out, it can be seen how the ten equally-weighed strands must be placed on the table.

At the start of the plaiting, for one plait, a whole bow, together with one strand from left and right have to be taken together. The strands should be kept fairly thick in the middle, to give a fine shape. A rosette, placed in the middle will serve to complete the star.

Plaiting scheme for basket-weave

Production of rosettes and roses

This style of plaiting serves in the main for the productinn of flat show-pieces. It is very simple to carry out. Care must be taken however that each strand is of the same thickness throughout and evenly plaited. The weaving should be carried out quickly. The dough should be kept covered with plastic as it is worked, so that it does not skin over.

The production is quite simple, as can be seen from the photograph of the work. Diameter of the cutter should be four to five cm.

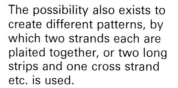

The possibility also exists to create different patterns, by which two strands each are plaited together, or two long strips and one cross strand etc. is used.

Fish

Mother's day heart

For the scales of the body a large lattice plait is made and this is then cut to the appropriate shape. The body should be enclosed top and bottom by two three-plaits. Shape the head and tail, put in place, and then divide from the body with a strip of dough. Fasten on the mouth and eye with egg wash.

The middle part, made of a basket weave is first produced and put on a sheet to prove. Only then is the three-part plait placed on around the heart shape. This plait must be made from very thin strands. Finally, decorate the Mother's day heart with a rose.

Grittibanzen and hares from zopf- or sweet dough

Even the historians are in the dark about the origins and stories of the Saint Nicholas bread, which are so loved both by adults as well as children. These dough shapes in human figures are only to be traced in Austria, Germany, Switzerland and Alsace over the past century. One knows nothing definite about their actual age: but the shape of the Solothurn Grittibanzen (the double pointed hat reminds one of the time of the Ambassadores) and gives a clue that it could have been known in the 18th century.

Grittibanzen made from zopf dough or sweet dough are signs of the present standard of living. Previously they were made of ordinary bread dough.

Dough

2000 g milk
200 g yeast
100 g Levit
40 g malt
40 g sugar
80 g salt
200 g eggs
3800 g whithe flour
600 g butter

Method

Break down the yeast, Levit, malt and sugar in the milk and mix with the flour. Mix the salt and egg together, add in stages and knead well to a pliable dough. Add the butter at the end. Bulk fermentation time is 15 minutes maximum.

184

Hares

Working off

Mould the dough pieces round, then out to longer shapes. At the blunt end turn about ¼ to form the head and place directly onto the sheet. Press the dough piece out a little flat and cut the arms and legs with a knife. After a full proof brush the Grittibanzen twice with egg and mark the eyes, nose and mouth with sultanas. Finally, bake in a moderate oven without steam, to a light colour.

Working off

First hand up the dough pieces round, and then mould them out to pear shapes. At the blunt end, twist about ¼ to form the head, and then press out flat. Then cut the arms, legs and ears using a knife. Place on a sheet and brush with egg. After a good proof brush again with egg and using a blade, mark in the various decorations as shown in the picture. Bake in a moderate oven without steam, to a light colour.

Animals from zopf dough

Flatten out zopf dough to about 10 mm thick, place on lightly dusted sheets and allow to stand for about 60 minutes in the deep freeze. Before working off, turn the pieces over so that a smooth surface is available for use. Put cardboard stencils on top and cut out the animal figures with a sharp knife. The pieces to be used for decoration are cut from the dough which has been flattened out to 5 mm thick. Put in place, brush with egg, allow to prove and brush again before baking. One may choose to cut decorations with scissors or a knife and it is then baked in a mild oven without steam.

Party-bread, party-rolls and bread figures

Dough

5 500 g water
  300 g yeast
  300 g Levit
  200 g salt
  300 g fat
5 000 g dark flour
2 000 g rye flour, half white
2 000 g coarse whole rye meal
      (fine)
1 500 g whole wheat flour

Method

Mix all of the ingredients, with
the exception of the fat and
salt, to a dough. The kneading
time in a spiral mixer will be
about 14 minutes in the first
gear. Add the fat when half
mixed and the salt at the end
of the mixing time. Allow to
ferment in bulk for 40 to 60
minutes.

Working off

Work off pieces of dough of
the desired size and mould
round or long, quite tightly.
Decorate with letters, figures
or any other desired inscrip-
tions. Finely dust the top with
flour and allow to prove in the
bakery, uncovered, for an
hour. Dock well before baking
so that there are no blisters or
holes in the top surface.
Baking temperature, according
to size, 220 to 230°C.

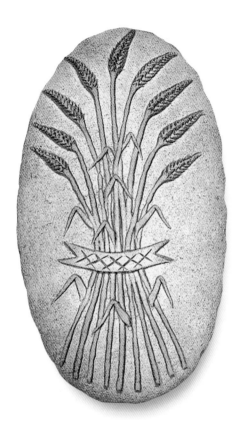

Small party breads

Taken from the small bread assortment, but reduced in weight to 20 to 30 g each, the party rolls complete the festive table perfectly, because of the variety and change that they can offer. Sandwiched with meat, sausage and cheese they gain in popularity for snacks between main meals as well as for parties and other festive occasions.

190

Tarts and flans

These have been standard items in the bakers and confectioners assortiment for many years. They offer many possibilities in the production of the many cakes and flans and their importance has increased in the past few years, and this trend will continue.

Flan paste or rubbed dough

Fruit tart with topping

1. Dough

1 000 g white flour
500 g butter
15 g salt
250 g water

Method

Rub the flour, butter and salt together. Add the water and mix to a paste.

2. Dough

1 000 g flour
500 g confectioners fat
15 g salt
250 g water

Method

Rub the flour, fat and salt together. Add the water, knead well and work off immediately. Allow to rest well before baking.

3. Dough

Rubbed dough with nuts
(Specially made for fruit tarts)

800 g white flour
200 g finely ground hazelnuts
500 g butter
15 g salt
250 g water

Method

As for dough 1.

Sweet fruit tart topping

1. Recipe

1 000 g milk
(or 800 g milk and
200 g cream)
200 g eggs
125 g sugar
120 g white flour

2. Recipe

600 g milk
400 g cream
200 g eggs
125 g sugar
125 g white flour
a little cinnamon

Fruit tarts without topping

Apple-, apricot-, cherry-, damson- and rhubarb tarts

Line a greased tin with the rubbed dough and dock. With fruit which has a lot of juice, it is recommended that the bottom is sprinkled with finely ground hazelnuts or sponge crumbs (they can also be used mixed). Decorate with the fruit and pour the topping over. Bake in a moderate oven. A little steam during baking will give an even colour to the top surface. A crisp base can be achieved by moving the tart around the oven a few times during its baking. When baked, remove the tart immediately from the tin and allow to cool on a wire.

Sprinkle some finely ground hazelnuts, sponge crumbs, flour dusting or a mixture of any of them in the bottom of a tin lined with the dough. Cover with a thicker layer of the fruits than would be the case for fruit tart with topping. Bake in a moderate oven without steam and eventually glaze. With sour fruits, such as rhubarb etc. sprinkle on a little sugar after baking.

Savoury flans

Cheese flans

Topping

1 000 g milk
     (or 800 g milk and
     200 g cream)
  200 g eggs
  120 g to 150 g
     white flour
   15 g spice mixture

Method

Mix together the eggs, flour
and seasoning. Add the milk,
or milk/cream a little at a time.

Spice mixture

1 000 g salt
   50 g pepper
   50 g nutmeg

Various reliable cheese mixture

½ Emmental + ½ Gruyere
= classical mixture
⅓ Emmental + ⅔ Gruyere
= slightly hot
All Gruyere
= spicy, hot

⅓ Sbrinz mixed into any of
the above mixtures makes
them light and aromatic.

For the topping with cheese
mixtures it is recommended to
mix them together for some
time in advance with the milk,
or at least to warm the milk to
60 to 70°C before mixing them
and then to stir the other
ingredients well through.

Method

1 cake of 30 cm diameter

350 g flan dough
250 g cheese mixture
500 g topping

Line a flan ring with rubbed
dough and dock. Cover with
the topping and bake in a
moderate oven with steam.
The steam helps the cheese to
melt on the top surface and
hinders any build up of a bitter
taste. Moving the flan around
the oven a few times during
the baking time will help to
give it a crispy bottom crust.
When baked, remove the flan
from the ring immediately and
place on a wire to cool.

Flan with visible topping

Decorations such as tomatoes,
mushrooms, herbs and such
like can be added after 10
minutes of the baking time so
that they will not sink to the
bottom completely, but will
still just be visible through the
topping.

194

Quiche Lorraine

Spinach-bacon flan

1 flan 30 cm diamater

Method

1 flan 30 cm diameter

350 g flan dough
150 g cheese mixture
200 g chopped onions
 30 g butter
120 g diced bacon
450 g topping

Finely chop the onions, dice the bacon and lightly cook them together in the butter. Then sprinkle it over the bottom of the lined flan, pour the topping and the cheese mixture on top and bake.

350 g flan dough
500 g leaf spinach
 80 g diced bacon
        spice mixture, nutmeg
 30 g butter
400 g topping
 40 g bacon slices, for topping

Pre-cook the spinach and drain well. Lightly cook the diced bacon and spice mixture in the butter. Sprinkle all onto the base of the flan, pour the topping over and the slices of bacon over the top. Bake in a good, hot, pre-steamed oven.

Pizza

Pizza à la mode du chef

Pizza Napolitana

1. Dough

Half-white bread dough, with 80 g oil per kg flour.

2. Dough

Weggli dough/puff pastry (with 2 turns, or puff pastry trimmings) 1 : 1
Give three single turns together.

Salsa-verde-seasoning

  75 g olive oil
  20 g parsley
  70 g anchovies
  50 g capers
     2 Garlic cloves
     Oregano, pepper, salt

Finely chop the parsley, anchovies and garlic and allow to cook a little with the other ingredients, in the oil.

350 g pizza dough
500 g tomato slices
150 g Fontina, melting cheese
     or Mozzarella
  30 g olives
  50 g peperoni
100 g ham
220 g Salsa-verde-seasoning

Cut the tomatoes and cheese into thin slices. Place the slices of tomato over the bottom of the lined flan ring, and the cheese slices on top. Sprinkle the chopped peperoni and strips of ham over the top and trickle the Salsa-verde-seasoning over that. Bake in a well heated, pre-steamed oven.

350 g pizza dough
200 g Mozzarella, Fontina or
     melting cheese
250 g tomato slices
  40 g anchovies
  40 g olives
  30 g oil
     Seasoning: Oregano,
     pepper, salt.

Cut the cheese and tomatoes into thin slices. Place the tomato on the bottom of the lined flan ring and the cheese slices over the top. Place the anchovies and olives on top and season. Finally, trickle the oil over the top and bake in a good, hot, pre-steamed oven.

Contents

Recipes